Web Applications with Go

Unlock the Power of Go for Real-World Web Server Development

Tommy Clark

Discover other books in the series

"Go Programming for Beginners: Master Go from Scratch with Easy-to-Follow Steps"

"System Programming with Go: Unlock the Power of System Calls, Networking, and Security with Practical Golang Projects"

"Go Programming for Microservices: Build Scalable, High-Performance Applications with Ease"

"Go Programming for Backend: The Developer's Blueprint for Efficiency and Performance"

"Web Security with Go: Build Safe and Resilient Applications"

"Network Automation with Go: Automate Network Operations and Build Scalable Applications with Go"

"Effective Debugging in Go: Master the Skills Every Go Developer"

Disclaimer

The information provided in "*Web Applications with Go: Unlock the Power of Go for Real-World Web Server Development*" by **Tommy Clark** is intended solely for educational and informational purposes. While every effort has been made to ensure the accuracy and completeness of the content, the author and publisher make no guarantees regarding the results that may be achieved by following the instructions or techniques described in this book.

Readers are encouraged to seek appropriate professional guidance for specific issues or challenges they may encounter, particularly in commercial or critical environments.

Introduction

Welcome to the course **"Web Applications with Go: Unlock the Power of Go for Real-World Web Server Development."** In a time when there is a greater need than ever for reliable, scalable, and effective web applications, the programming language you choose has a significant impact on the outcome of your projects. Go, sometimes referred to as Golang, has gained popularity because to its powerful concurrency model, beautiful simplicity, and efficiency.

What makes Go a unique option for web development might be on your mind. Google developers created Go, which emphasizes simplicity to boost productivity without compromising the strength and adaptability required for sophisticated web applications. It is an excellent choice for creating dependable and quick online services that can support thousands of concurrent users due to its statically typed architecture and garbage collection features.

We will explore web application development using Go in great detail in this book. Our objective is to give you the skills and resources you need to create practical web servers and apps that are not only effective but also scalable and maintained, regardless of your level of programming   experience.

We will begin by going over the basic ideas of Go programming, including its distinct syntax and salient characteristics. After that, we'll move on to more useful applications, looking at how to use the built-in net/http package to build web servers, comprehend RESTful architecture, and use middleware to improve your web apps.

Along the way, we'll also go over best practices, investigate different frameworks and libraries to increase the functionality of your apps, and examine real-world case studies that showcase Go's advantages. You will have a strong foundation in Go web programming and the self-assurance to create, implement, and manage high-performing web apps by the end of this book.

Therefore, Go provides a multitude of opportunities and innovation at your fingertips, regardless of whether you're working on a tiny personal project or trying to create enterprise-level online apps. Let's go off on this thrilling adventure to realize your ideas and realize Go's full potential for web server development!

Chapter 1: Go Programming Language Fundamentals

The open-source programming language Go, sometimes referred to as Golang, was created at Google by Ken Thompson, Rob Pike, and Robert Griesemer. It was developed to solve issues with other programming languages, especially those related to simplicity of use, scalability, and concurrency. Developers have been using Go for system programming, web development, cloud services, and other purposes since its initial release in 2009.

The basic ideas of the Go programming language, including its special features, syntax, data types, control structures, functions, and modules, will be discussed in this chapter. You ought to have a firm grasp of Go's fundamentals by the end of this chapter and be ready to create basic programs.

##1.1 Go's Distinctive Qualities

Efficiency and Simplicity

Simplicity is one of the fundamental design principles of Go. Because of the language's simple syntax, developers may create software without the complications that come with using other programming languages. Go is appropriate for high-performance applications since it places an emphasis on effective execution.

Concurrency

Go uss goroutines and channels to present a potent concurrency paradigm.

Developers can perform several tasks at once via goroutines, which are lightweight threads, and channels, which provide communication and synchronization between goroutines. Writing programs that fully utilize contemporary multi-core computers is made simple by this.

Typing Statically and Powerfully

Because Go is statically typed, variable types are verified after compilation rather than during execution. Better performance is made possible, and type-related errors are less likely to occur. However, Go is tightly typed, which eliminates uncertainty in code by preventing implicit type conversions.

Garbage Collection Go has an effective garbage collector that controls memory reclaim and allocation automatically. By reducing the need for developers to manually manage memory and preventing memory leaks, this improves code safety and productivity.

1.2 Setting Up the Development Environment

Before diving into Go, it's essential to set up a suitable development environment.

Install Go: Visit golang.org and download the latest version of Go suitable for your operating system. Follow the instructions to install it.

Set Up Your Workspace: Create a workspace directory where all your Go projects will reside. Go uses a specific directory structure, so it's important to understand how it fits into your workflow.

Configure Your Path: Ensure that your Go installation directory (usually `$GOROOT/bin`) is added to your system's PATH environment variable. This allows you to run the `go` command from any terminal window.

Choose an Editor: While you can use any text editor, several IDEs and editors support Go natively, such as Visual Studio Code, GoLand, and Atom. Choose one that fits your preferences for syntax highlighting, code completion, and debugging features.

1.3 Basic Syntax in Go

Go has a straightforward syntax, making it easy to read and write. Here are some fundamental aspects: ### Hello, World!
Let's start with the classic "Hello, World!" program. Create a file named `hello.go`.

```go
package main
import "fmt" func main(){
fmt.Println("Hello, World!")
}
```

Explanation:
The `package main` line declares that this file is part of the `main` package, which is the starting point of any Go application.
The `import "fmt"` statement imports the `fmt` package, which contains functions for formatted I/O.
The `main` function is the entry point of the program. `fmt.Println` outputs text to the console. ### Variables and Data Types
Go supports several built-in data types, including:

- **Integers**: `int`, `int8`, `int16`, `int32`, `int64`
Floats: `float32`, `float64`
Booleans: `bool`
Strings: `string`

Declaring variables in Go can be done using the `var` keyword or shorthand `:=` syntax.

```go
var age int = 30 name := "Alice"
```

Control Structures

Go provides standard control structures like `if`, `for`,

and `switch`.#### If Statements

```go
if age >= 18 {
fmt.Println(name, "is an adult.")
} else {
fmt.Println(name, "is a minor.")
}
```

For Loop

Go has a single looping construct — the `for` loop.

```go
for i := 0; i < 5; i++ {fmt.Println(i)
}
```

Switch Statement

The `switch` statement is a convenient way to select from multiple alternatives.

```go
switch day := "Monday"; day {case "Monday":
fmt.Println("Start of the week.")case "Friday":
fmt.Println("End of the week.")default:
fmt.Println("Middle of the week.")
}
```

1.4 Functions in Go

Functions in Go are first-class citizens, meaning they can be assigned to variables, passed as arguments, and returned from other functions.

Defining a Function

```go
func add(a int, b int) int {return a + b
}
```

Calling a Function

```go
result := add(5, 3) fmt.Println("The sum is:", result)
```

Variadic Functions

You can define functions that take a variable number of arguments using ellipsis (`...`).

```go
func sum(nums ...int) int {total := 0
for _, num := range nums {total += num
}
return total
}
```

1.5 Packages and Modules

Go organizes code into packages. A package is a collection of related Go files. You can create a package by defining a directory of `.go` files with a common `package` statement.

Creating a Module

Modules are Go's way of managing dependencies. To create a module:

Open a terminal in your project directory.
Run `go mod init module-name`.

This creates a `go.mod` file which will track your project's dependencies.

In this chapter, we explored the fundamental features of the Go programming language, including its syntax, variable declaration, control structures, functions, and package management. You should now have a basic understanding of how to set up your development environment and write simple Go programs.

As we progress through this book, we'll dive deeper into more advanced topics, such as concurrency, testing, and web development with Go. With the foundation laid here, you are well-equipped to continue your journey into the world of Go programming.

Core Syntax and Language Features in GO

Its simplicity, efficiency, and powerful concurrency

capabilities make it an increasingly popular choice for system programming, web development, and cloud services. This chapter delves into the core syntax and language features of Go, providing a solid foundation for understanding and effectively using the language.

1. Basic Syntax

1.1 Structure of a Go Program

A Go program is organized into packages. The `main` package is special because it defines the entry point for the application. Each Go file typically begins with a `package` declaration, followed by `import` statements for importing other packages, and ends with one or more functions.

```go
package mainimport "fmt"
func main() { fmt.Println("Hello, World!")
}
```

In this example, the code imports the `fmt` package, which contains formatting functions, and it defines a `main` function that serves as the program's entry point.
1.2 Comments
Go supports single-line and multi-line comments:

```go
// This is a single-line comment

/*
```

This is a multi-line comment.It can span multiple lines.
*/
```

Comments are an essential part of writing clear, maintainable code, and Go encourages their use. ## 2. Variables and Data Types
### 2.1 Variable Declaration

In Go, you can declare variables using the `var` keyword. You can also use shorthand notation (`:=`) for implicit type declaration.

```go
var x int = 10        // Explicit declarationy := 20      // Implicit declaration

```

You can also declare multiple variables in a single statement:

```go
var a, b, c int = 1, 2, 3
d, e := 4, 5
```

2.2 Data Types

Go has several built-in data types, including:

Booleans: `bool`
- **Numbers**: `int`, `int8`, `int16`, `int32`, `int64`,
```

`uint`, `uint8`, `uint16`, `uint32`, `uint64`, `float32`, `float64`, `complex64`, `complex128`
Strings: `string`
Arrays and Slices
Maps
Structs

The type system is strong and static, meaning types are checked at compile time, reducing errors and improving code safety.

3. Control Structures

Go's control structures include `if`, `for`, and `switch`, which provide the primary means of controlling the flow of a program.

3.1 Conditional Statements

The `if` statement in Go is straightforward:

```go
x := 10
if x < 0 { fmt.Println("Negative")
} else {
fmt.Println("Non-negative")
}
```

You can also declare variables in the `if` statement itself:

```go
if y := 10; y > 5 {
```

```go
    fmt.Println("y is greater than 5")
}
```

3.2 Loops

Go only has a `for` loop, but it is versatile. You can use it in several forms:

```go
// Traditional for loopfor i := 0; i < 5; i++ {
fmt.Println(i)
}

// While-style loopj := 0
for j < 5 { fmt.Println(j)j++
}

// Infinite loopfor {
fmt.Println("This will run forever")
}
```

3.3 Switch Statements

The `switch` statement provides a cleaner alternative to multiple `if-else` statements:

```go day := 3
switch day {case 1:
fmt.Println("Monday")case 2:
fmt.Println("Tuesday")case 3:
fmt.Println("Wednesday")default:
```

```go
    fmt.Println("Other day")
}
```

4. Functions and Methods### 4.1 Defining Functions

Functions in Go are defined using the `func` keyword. You can specify parameters and return types:

```go
func add(a int, b int) int {return a + b
}
```

You can also return multiple values, a common paradigm in Go:

```go
func divide(a, b int) (int, int) {return a / b, a % b

}
```

4.2 Methods

Methods in Go are functions with a special receiver argument. This feature enables object-oriented programming styles:

```go
type Rectangle struct {width, height int
}

func (r Rectangle) area() int {return r.width * r.height
```

```go
}

rect := Rectangle{width: 10, height: 5}fmt.Println("Area:",
rect.area())
```

5. Concurrency

One of Go's standout features is its built-in support for
concurrency through goroutines and channels. ### 5.1
Goroutines
A goroutine is a lightweight thread managed by the Go
runtime. You can start a goroutine simply by using the
`go` keyword:

```go
go func() {
fmt.Println("Executing in a goroutine")
}()
```

5.2 Channels

Channels are used to communicate between goroutines.
They can be created using the `make` function:

```go
ch := make(chan int)

go func() {
ch <- 42 // Send value to channel
}()
```

```
value := <-ch // Receive value from channel
fmt.Println(value)
```

Channels ensure safe communication between goroutines, helping to prevent race conditions.

Understanding variables, control structures, functions, methods, and concurrency constructs helps developers harness the language's power. Go's emphasis on simplicity and clarity makes it a compelling choice for both new and experienced programmers. As you continue your journey with Go, the topics covered here willserve as essential building blocks for more complex programming tasks and software development projects.

Building and Running Go Programs in GO

Created at Google by Robert Griesemer, Rob Pike, and Ken Thompson, Go has gained popularity for its performance and built-in support for concurrent programming. This chapter will guide you through the process of building and running Go programs, covering essential concepts, tools, and best practices.

Setting Up the Go Environment

Before you can build and run Go programs, you need to set up your development environment. Followthesesteps to get started:

Install Go:
Download the latest version of Go from the official Go

website (https://golang.org/dl/).
Follow the installation instructions appropriate for your operating system (Windows, macOS, or Linux).
Verify the installation by running `go version` in your terminal. You should see the Go version youinstalled.

Set upthe Go Workspace:
Go uses a workspace structure to organize your projects. The default workspace is typically located at `$HOME/go`.
Within the workspace, you have three main directories:
`src`: contains the source code of your Go programs.
`pkg`: contains compiled package objects.
`bin`: contains executable binaries.

You can customize your workspace path by setting the `GOPATH` environment variable, although with Go Modules, a module-based approach is now common.

Creating Your First Go Program

Let's walk through creating a simple Go program. Follow these steps:

Create a New Go Project:
- Navigate to your workspace source directory:
```bash
cd $HOME/go/src
```

- Create a new directory for your project:
```bash
mkdir hello-gocd hello-go
```

Write Your Go Code:
- Create a new file named `main.go` using your favorite text editor:
```go
package mainimport "fmt"

func main() { fmt.Println("Hello, World!")
}
```

Understanding the Code:
The `package main` statement defines the package name. The `main` package is special in Go; it tells the Go compiler that this package should compile as an executable program.
The `import "fmt"` statement allows us to use the `fmt` package, which provides formatted I/O functions.
The `main()` function is the entry point of the program where execution starts.## Building Go Programs
Building a Go program compiles your source code into an executable binary. Here's how to do it:

Build the Program:
In your terminal, ensure you are in the project directory (`hello-go`), then run:
```bash go build
```

This command creates an executable file named `hello-go` (or `hello-go.exe` on Windows) in the current directory.

Running the Built Executable:

- To run the program, execute:
```bash
./hello-go
```

- You should see the output:
```plaintext Hello, World!
```

Alternatively, you can run your program directly without building it first, using the following command:

```bash
go run main.go
```

This command compiles and runs the program in one step. It's useful for quick testing and development. ## Managing Dependencies with Go Modules
As projects grow, they often rely on external libraries. Go Modules provide a way to manage these dependencies easily.

Initialize a Go Module:
- Inside your project directory, run:
```bash
go mod init hello-go
```

- This command creates a `go.mod` file, which will manage your project's dependencies.

Adding Dependencies:
- If you want to use a third-party library, you can import it in your code. For example:

```go
import "github.com/gorilla/mux"
```

After modifying your code, run:
```bash
go get
```

This command fetches the necessary dependencies and updates the `go.mod` and `go.sum` files.

Building and Running with Modules:
- You can build and run your program as before. The Go toolchain automatically uses the `go.mod` file to manage dependencies.

Debugging Go Programs

Debugging is a critical part of development, and Go provides various tools for this purpose.

Using the Go Tool:
- The `go test` command helps you test your code by running the test files you create. For instance, create a file named `main_test.go`:
```go
package main import "testing"
func TestMain(t *testing.T) { result := someFunction()
expected := "expected result"if result != expected {
t.Errorf("Expected %s, but got %s", expected, result)
}
}
```

- Run your tests with:
```bash
go test
```

```

```

Delve:
For advanced debugging, consider using Delve, a Go debugger. Install it by following the instructions on its GitHub repository (https://github.com/go-delve/delve).
Run your program with Delve to set breakpoints and inspect variables.

In this chapter, we explored how to build and run Go programs, from setting up your environment to managing dependencies and debugging. Go's simplicity and powerful tooling make it an excellent choice for both beginners and experienced developers. As you continue your journey in Go, remember to leverage the community, seek out libraries for common tasks, and maintain best practices in your coding approach. The world of Go is rich and vibrant, and you're now equipped to dive deeper!

Chapter 2: Advanced Go Concepts and Techniques

This chapter will delve into sophisticated strategies, tactical maneuvers, and deeper understanding of concepts that transcend the basics. By mastering these elements, players can unlock the subtleties and nuances of Go, creating a more profound engagement with this ancient art.

2.1 The Importance of Shape

In Go, "shape" refers to the configuration of stones on the board, which can significantly impact both local and global strategies. A good shape allows for efficient use of stones, maximizing territory while minimizing weaknesses. Here are some essential shapes to recognize and employ:

2.1.1 Good Shapes

Tigers Mouth: This shape resembles a tiger's mouth and offers strong connections while being difficult for opponents to attack. It provides safety and potential for further expansion.

Ponnuki: Formed when capturing stones, ponnuki is a strong shape that tends to yield influence and territory. Its usefulness extends far beyond the immediate area of influence, often acting as a springboard for attacks.

Kikashi: A tactic that involves making a move (often a sacrifice) that forces your opponent to respond, ultimately allowing you to gain more advantageous positions afterward.

2.1.2 Weak Shapes

Understanding bad shapes is just as crucial as recognizing good ones. Shapes like the "empty triangle" or "slack four" can lead to vulnerabilities and give an opponent leverage over you. A focus on minimizing these weaknesses will enhance defensive capabilities and strategic acumen.

2.2 Balancing Territory and Influence

One of the core strategic dilemmas in Go is the balance between territory and influence. Players must decide when to prioritize solid territory and when to build influence, which may not yield immediate points but can lead to a stronger board position.

2.2.1 Territory

Territory is a direct measure of victory in Go. To secure territory, players should focus on creating large, enclosed areas while also being mindful of not spreading themselves too thin. Recognizing potential areas for enclosement and proactively positioning stones to fortify those claims is key.

2.2.2 Influence

Influence governs the overall control of the board, granting players the ability to challenge their opponent's position more effectively. While secure territory provides immediate points, strong influence can turn the tide in future battles.

2.2.3 The Dichotomy

The art of Go involves constantly evaluating this balance. Sometimes, a move focused on influence allows a player to push for a future territory gain. In contrast, other moves may need to secure immediate points, leading to crucial decisions during gameplay.

2.3 Life and Death

Understanding life-and-death situations is fundamental to advanced Go play. Whether a group of stones can be considered "alive" (secured) or "dead" (captured) will dictate major shifts in strategy.

2.3.1 Living Groups

A group is considered alive if it can secure at least two eyes, or independent empty spaces, allowing the group to survive against attacks. Players must analyze their groups throughout the game, ensuring they maintain sufficient eye space while also threatening their opponent's groups.

2.3.2 Dead Groups

Recognizing when a group is dead is essential. Players should aggressively seek to cut off and capture dead groups, as each captured stone adds to their score. Engaging in fighting skills and reading the board impacts the outcome significantly.

2.4 Advanced Tactical Plays

Advanced Go is not just about understanding shapes and strength; it's also about the tactics and tactical plays that can decisively change the momentum of the game.

2.4.1 Sabaki

Sabaki is a technique used to simplify a complex group of stones, often involving reducing the strength of an opponent's influence or territory. This strategic maneuvering is a hallmark of skilled players who can adapt to rapidly changing board dynamics.

2.4.2 Ko Fights

Ko is a unique aspect of Go that allows for cyclical capturing. Fights for ko can yield vital changes in the overall board positioning, and players often must weigh the risks and rewards of engaging in such a battle.

2.4.3 Semeai (Ladder Battles)

Engaging in semeai, or capturing races, tests a player's ability to read the board and predict outcomes. Mastering these sequences helps develop an intuitive sense of timing and spatial awareness that are crucial for effective Go play.

The journey to mastering Go is a continuous one filled with learning and adaptation. As players explore these advanced concepts and techniques—shapes, balance between territory and influence, life and death situations, and tactical plays—they will develop a richer understanding of the game.

Goroutines and Concurrency in Go

The Go programming language, known for its simplicity and efficiency, introduces a unique model for handling concurrency through Goroutines and Channels. In this chapter, we will dive into the core conceptsof Goroutines, concurrency management, and how Go's design facilitates writing effective concurrent programs.

Understanding Goroutines

At the heart of Go's concurrency model is the Goroutine. A Goroutine is a lightweight thread of execution, managed by the Go runtime. Creating a Goroutine is as simple as prefixing a function call with the `go` keyword. This allows the function to run asynchronously, freeing up the main program to continue executingwithout waiting for the Goroutine to complete.

Example of Goroutines

Here's a simple example of how to use Goroutines in Go:

```go
package main

import ("fmt"
"time"
)
```

```go
func sayHello() {
for i := 0; i < 5; i++ { fmt.Println("Hello from Goroutine")
time.Sleep(time.Second)
}
}

func main() {
go sayHello() // Start the Goroutinefor i := 0; i < 5; i++ {
fmt.Println("Hello from Main")time.Sleep(time.Second)
}
}
```
```

In this example, when `go sayHello()` is called, the program starts executing `sayHello()` concurrently with the `main()` function. As a result, both "Hello from Goroutine" and "Hello from Main" messages will be printed at roughly the same time.

### How Goroutines Work

Goroutines are extremely lightweight compared to traditional OS threads. While creating a thread can be resource-intensive, Goroutines are managed by the Go runtime, which multiplexes multiple Goroutines onto a smaller number of OS threads. This efficient management allows you to run thousands of Goroutinessimultaneously without incurring significant overhead. ## Synchronization and Communication
While Goroutines enable concurrent execution, they also introduce challenges related to synchronization anddata sharing. When multiple Goroutines access shared
```

resources simultaneously, it can lead to race conditions where the outcome depends on the timing of the execution.

Channels: A Concurrency Primitive

To facilitate communication and synchronization between Goroutines, Go provides Channels. Channels allow Goroutines to communicate with each other by sending and receiving values. They are a safe way to share data among Goroutines, allowing one Goroutine to send data and another to receive it.

Basic Channel Usage

Here's how to create and use a Channel in Go:

```go
package main

import ("fmt"
)

func sendData(ch chan<- string) { ch <- "Hello from Channel"
}

func main() {
messageChannel := make(chan string) // Create a Channel

go sendData(messageChannel) // Start a Goroutine to send data
```

```go
    message := <-messageChannel // Receive data from the
    Channel fmt.Println(message) // Output: Hello from
    Channel
}
```

In this code, the main function creates a Channel named `messageChannel` and passes it to the `sendData` Goroutine. The `sendData` function sends a message to the channel, which is then received in the main function.

Buffered vs. Unbuffered Channels Channels can be either buffered or unbuffered.
Unbuffered Channels: These require both a sender and a receiver to be ready at the same time. The sending Goroutine will block until another Goroutine is ready to receive the data.

Buffered Channels: These allow you to specify a capacity when creating a channel. The sender can send multiple values to the channel without blocking until it has filled the capacity, at which point it will block until a receiver is ready.

```go
bufferedChannel := make(chan string, 3) // Create a buffered Channel with a capacity of 3
```

Select Statement

The `select` statement provides a way to wait on multiple

Channel operations. It can be particularly useful for handling timeouts or dealing with multiple Goroutines simultaneously.

```go
select {
case msg := <-ch1: fmt.Println("Received:", msg)
case msg := <-ch2: fmt.Println("Received:", msg)
case        <-time.After(5        *        time.Second):
fmt.Println("Timeout!")
}
```

In this example, the `select` block waits for messages from either `ch1` or `ch2`. If neither channel sends a message within a specified timeout, it executes the fallback case.

Error Handling in Concurrent Programs

When working with concurrency, error handling becomes crucial. Goroutines can fail independently, and handling errors effectively requires careful design. One common pattern is to use a combination of Channels and Goroutines to pass errors back to the main program:

```go
func worker(id int, ch chan int, errCh chan error) {
// Simulate some workif id%2 == 0 {
errCh <- fmt.Errorf("worker %d encountered an error", id)return
}
ch <- id
}
```

```
func main() {
ch := make(chan int) errCh := make(chan error)for i := 0;
i < 10; i++ {
go worker(i, ch, errCh)
}

for i := 0; i < 10; i++ {select {
case msg := <-ch: fmt.Println("Received worker:", msg)
case err := <-errCh: fmt.Println("Error:", err)
}
}

}
```

In this example, if a worker encounters an error, it sends the error through `errCh`. The main function uses `select` to handle both successful messages and errors gracefully.

Goroutines and Channels form the cornerstone of concurrency in Go. They provide a simple yet powerful way to write concurrent programs without the complexity of traditional threading models. By leveraging Goroutines for asynchronous execution and Channels for communication, developers can create responsive, efficient, and maintainable concurrent applications.

Handling Errors and Panic/Recover Mechanisms

This chapter delves into error handling, with a specific focus on panic/recover mechanisms commonly found in programming languages, notably in Go. We will explore various types of errors, strategies for handling them, and how panic/recover can be effectively utilized to maintain the stability of an application.

Understanding Errors

Errors can be broadly categorized into two types: compile-time errors and runtime errors.### Compile-time Errors These occur during the compilation of the code. They include syntax errors, type mismatches, and any issues that a compiler can identify. Debugging these errors is usually more straightforward since the compiler provides feedback directly related to the line of code causing the problem.

Runtime Errors

Runtime errors occur while the program is executing. Unlike compile-time errors, these can arise from unforeseen circumstances, such as:

Invalid user input
Resource unavailability (e.g., file not found)
Division by zero
Out-of-bounds access in arrays or slices ### Panic vs. Recover
One of the distinctive features of Go is its approach to error handling, particularly the concepts of "panic" and "recover." Let's explore these mechanisms in detail.

Panic

In Go, a panic is a built-in function that is executed when a program encounters a critical error or an unexpected condition that it cannot recover from. When a panic occurs, the normal execution flow is disrupted, and the program begins to unwind the stack. This effectively halts the execution of the current goroutine, allowing you to log error messages and execute clean-up tasks.

When to Use Panic

Panic is typically reserved for scenarios where the program cannot continue safely. Examples include:

Attempting to access a nil pointer
Failing to open a necessary resource
Invariant violations (i.e., when an assumption made by the code is proven false)

While panic can help diagnose issues during development, it should be used sparingly in production code, as it can lead to unpredictable behavior and difficulty in maintaining the code.

Recover

Recover is a built-in function that provides a way to regain control of a panicking goroutine. It allows developers to handle the panic gracefully, resuming normal execution. However, recover can only be called within a deferred function, which gives it its unique characteristics.

How to Use Recover

Defer the Function: Declare the recover call within a deferred function to ensure it can catch any panics that occur in the surrounding function.

Check for Panic: Call recover to retrieve the panic value. If it returns nil, there was no panic; if it returns a non-nil value, you can handle the error accordingly.

Example
```go
package main

import (
"errors""fmt"
)

func riskyFunction() {defer func() {
if r := recover(); r != nil { fmt.Println("Recovered from panic:", r)
}
}()

// This will cause a panicvar a *int
*a = 1 // Dereferencing a nil pointer
}

func main() { riskyFunction()
fmt.Println("Program continues after recovery.")
}
```

In the above code, the `riskyFunction` may panic when trying to dereference a nil pointer, but thanks to the

`recover`, we can handle the situation gracefully, allowing the program to continue executing. ## Best Practices for Error Handling
Return Errors Appropriately: Functions that can encounter errors should return an error as the second return value. This practice allows the caller to decide how to handle the error.

Use Panic Sparingly: Reserve panic for unrecoverable situations, and avoid panicking on regular error conditions. Get accustomed to returning appropriate error values instead.

Log or Handle Errors: Always log or appropriately handle the errors returned by functions to ensure that they do not propagate unhandled.

Contextual Error Messages: Whenever possible, make your error messages descriptive. This aids in debugging and understanding the root cause of issues.

Testing: Implement unit tests to cover potential error cases. Testing your error handling code can help ensure robustness.

Effective error handling is a cornerstone of reliable software development. By strategically using mechanisms like panic and recover, developers can create applications that gracefully handle errors, leading to improved user experiences and easier maintenance. As we continue to explore the intricacies of programming, embracing best practices in error management will empower developers to write resilient and robust applications.

Understanding errors and implementing appropriate handling strategies are essential skills for any developer. As you move forward in your programming journey, remember that how you handle errors is not just about mitigating problems but also about ensuring a seamless experience for users.

Chapter 3: Understanding Web Servers

A web server is more than just a physical machine; it's a vital component that bridges the gap between users and the data they seek. In this chapter, we will explore the anatomy of web servers, their types, roles, and the technologies that power them.

3.1 What is a Web Server?

At its core, a web server is a system that stores, processes, and delivers web pages to clients. These clients are typically web browsers, but they can also be other devices like mobile phones, tablets, or even applications. When you type a URL into your browser, you issue a request to the web server hosting the website, which then responds by sending back the requested webpage, usually in the form of HTML, CSS, and JavaScript files.

3.1.1 How Web Servers Work

The communication between a client and a server follows the request-response model. Here's a simplified overview of this process:

Client Request: The user enters a URL in the browser's address bar. This prompts the browser to send an HTTP request to the web server identified by the URL.

DNS Resolution: Before the request reaches the server, the browser translates the human-readable URL into an IP address via the Domain Name System (DNS).

Processing the Request: Once the server receives the request, it processes it, which may involve accessing databases, running server-side scripts, or fetching other resources.

Server Response: The server then sends back an HTTP response containing the requested resourcesor an error message if the request could not be fulfilled.

Rendering the Content: Finally, the web browser renders the web page for the user to view.## 3.2 Types of Web Servers
Web servers can be categorized based on various aspects, including functionality, platform, and the technologies they support.

3.2.1 Static vs. Dynamic Web Servers

Static Web Servers: These servers deliver fixed content that does not change based on user interactionor requests. The files (HTML, CSS, and images) are pre-stored, and the server simply sends them to the client when requested. Examples include Apache HTTP Server and Nginx.

Dynamic Web Servers: Unlike static servers, dynamic servers generate web content on the fly. They typically interface with databases and server-side scripting languages (like PHP, Python, or Ruby) to deliver personalized or updated content. Well-known dynamic servers include Microsoft IIS and Apache Tomcat.

3.2.2 Dedicated vs. Shared Web Servers

Dedicated Web Servers: These servers are exclusively allocated to a single user or organization. They provide high performance, enhanced security, and full control over the server's configurations. Dedicated servers are ideal for high-traffic websites that require significant resources.

Shared Web Servers: In contrast, shared servers host multiple websites on the same physical server. While this option is cost-effective, it can lead to performance issues if one site's resource usage impacts others. Shared hosting is a common choice for small businesses and personal websites.

3.2.3 Virtual and Cloud Servers

Virtual Servers: These servers partition physical hardware into multiple virtual instances, allowing multiple users to operate their own servers with allocated resources. This flexibility often leads to cost savings and efficient resource management.

Cloud Servers: Leveraging cloud computing technology, cloud servers provide scalable resources and functionality through the internet. They offer on-demand computing power and storage, allowing businesses to adapt quickly to changing demands.

3.3 Key Web Server Technologies

Understanding the technologies that underpin web servers is essential for recognizing their capabilities and limits.

3.3.1 HTTP Protocol

HTTP (Hypertext Transfer Protocol) is the foundation of data communication on the web. It defines howmessages are formatted and transmitted and how servers and browsers respond to various commands.
Understanding HTTP is crucial for optimizing web server performance and troubleshooting issues. ### 3.3.2 Web Server Software
The software running on a web server determines how it interacts with clients and processes requests.Popular web server software includes:

Apache HTTP Server: Open-source and widely used, Apache supports various operating systems andis known for its flexibility and extensive module ecosystem.

Nginx: Known for its efficiency and speed, Nginx is particularly adept at handling concurrentconnections and is commonly used as a reverse proxy server.

Microsoft Internet Information Services (IIS): A web server for Windows environments, IIS integrates seamlessly with other Microsoft services and technologies.

3.3.3 Security Measures

Security is a paramount concern for web servers, given their exposure to potential threats. Web servers often implement measures such as SSL/TLS encryption for secure data transmission, firewalls to control incoming and outgoing traffic, and regular updates to safeguard against vulnerabilities.

In summary, web servers are fundamental to the functioning of the internet, acting as the bridge for communication between users and the content they seek. Understanding the types and functions of web servers, as well as the technologies that drive them, is crucial for anyone venturing into the digital realm. As our reliance on web services continues to grow, so too does the importance of mastering the principles of web server operation, performance optimization, and security.

HTTP Request and Response Cycle

This protocol facilitates communication between clients (typically web browsers) and servers (where web content is stored). Understanding the HTTP request and response cycle is essential for grasping how web applications operate. This chapter will explore the components of this cycle, its underlying mechanics, and its significance in web development.

1. The Foundation of HTTP

HTTP operates as a request-response protocol housed within the application layer of the Internet protocol suite. It is designed for transferring hypertext documents, allowing users to interact with web content seamlessly. At its core, HTTP is stateless, meaning each request from a client to a server is treated as an independent transaction, with no memory of previous exchanges.

2. The HTTP Request Cycle

The HTTP request cycle begins with a client initiating a request to the server. This cycle can be broken down into several steps:

2.1. Establishing a Connection

Before a request can be sent, the client must establish a connection to the server. This is typically done using TCP (Transmission Control Protocol). After the client types a URL into the browser, the browser resolves the domain name into an IP address through the Domain Name System (DNS) and initiates a TCP handshake with the server.

2.2. Crafting the Request

Once a connection is established, the client formulates an HTTP request. An HTTP request consists of several components:

Request Method: This indicates the action the client wants the server to perform. Common methods include:
`GET`: Requests data from a specified resource.
`POST`: Submits data to be processed to a specified resource.
`PUT`: Updates a specific resource.
`DELETE`: Removes a specified resource.

Request URL: The specific resource identified by the client's request, such as a webpage or image.

HTTP Version: The version of the HTTP protocol being used (e.g., HTTP/1.1, HTTP/2).

Headers: These provide additional information to the server, including metadata about the request, authentication tokens, content types, and client information.

Body: This is optional and exists primarily in `POST` and `PUT` requests, containing any data the client wishes to send to the server.

2.3. Sending the Request

After crafting the request, the client sends it to the server over the established TCP connection. The server listens for requests on a specific port (usually port 80 for HTTP and port 443 for HTTPS) and processes incoming requests accordingly.

3. The HTTP Response Cycle

Once the server receives and processes the client's request, it formulates an appropriate response. The HTTP response cycle includes the following steps:

3.1. Processing the Request

Upon receipt of the request, the server performs various tasks based on the request type. This might involve querying a database, retrieving files, or performing computations. The server's application logic generates a response based on the input received.

3.2. Crafting the Response

The server constructs the HTTP response, which consists of several key components:

HTTP Status Code: This is a three-digit number indicating the outcome of the request. Common status codes include:
`200 OK`: The request was successfully processed.
`404 Not Found`: The requested resource could not be found.
`500 Internal Server Error`: An unexpected error occurred on the server.

Headers: Similar to the request headers, response headers contain metadata about the response, such as the content type, content length, server information, and caching directives.

Body: The body of the response contains the data requested by the client, such as HTML content, JSON data, or images.

3.3. Sending the Response

The server sends the crafted response back to the client over the existing TCP connection. The client receives the response, which it processes for display.

4. Closing the Connection

After the response is sent, the TCP connection may

remain open for a brief period (for further requests) or may be closed immediately. HTTP/1.1 introduced persistent connections, allowing multiple requests and responses to be sent over a single connection, enhancing efficiency.

4.1. Persistent vs. Non-Persistent Connections

Non-Persistent Connection: The connection is closed after a single request-response cycle. Each new request opens a new connection, leading to increased latency due to the overhead of establishing multiple connections.

Persistent Connection: The connection remains open for multiple requests and responses, reducing latency and resource consumption by reusing the same connection.

The HTTP request and response cycle is the backbone of web communication. Understanding this cycle helps developers create robust applications and diagnose issues effectively. By grasping the mechanisms of HTTP requests, responses, and status codes, one can harness the full potential of web technologies.

Middleware in Go Web Applications

In the context of Go (Golang) web applications, middleware serves as an intermediary between the request and response cycle. It allows developers to inject functionality into the request processing pipeline, thus enhancing the application's performance, maintainability, and security.

Middleware can perform a variety of tasks such as logging requests, authenticating users, compressing responses, and serving static files. This chapter explores the implementation of middleware in Go web applications, examining how it can be effectively utilized to manage different aspects of web requests and responses.

The Role of Middleware in Go

In Go, middleware functions are typically defined as functions that take an `http.Handler` as a parameter and return another `http.Handler`. This design pattern allows for the composition of multiple middleware layers, each of which can add its functionality.

Here's a simple middleware function structure:

```go
func Middleware(next http.Handler) http.Handler {
return http.HandlerFunc(func(w http.ResponseWriter, r *http.Request) {
// Pre-processing logic before handling the request
next.ServeHTTP(w, r) // Call the next middleware/handler
// Post-processing logic after handling the request
})
}
```

The example above demonstrates a basic middleware that surrounds the handler with pre and post-processing logic. The `next` handler is called to continue the request processing.

Typical Use Cases for Middleware ### 1. Logging

Middleware is often used for logging requests and responses. By logging incoming requests, developers can track usage patterns and diagnose issues more easily. A logging middleware might look something like this:

```go
func LoggingMiddleware(next http.Handler) http.Handler {
return http.HandlerFunc(func(w http.ResponseWriter, r *http.Request) { log.Printf("Incoming request: %s %s", r.Method, r.URL.Path) next.ServeHTTP(w, r)
log.Printf("Response sent for: %s %s", r.Method, r.URL.Path)
})
}
```

2. Authentication

Another common use for middleware is authentication. A middleware can check if a user is authenticated before allowing access to certain routes or resources.

```go
func AuthenticationMiddleware(next http.Handler) http.Handler {
return http.HandlerFunc(func(w http.ResponseWriter, r *http.Request) {token := r.Header.Get("Authorization")
if token != "expected-token" {
http.Error(w, "Unauthorized", http.StatusUnauthorized)
return
```

```
    }
    next.ServeHTTP(w, r)
  })
}
```

3. CORS Handling

Cross-Origin Resource Sharing (CORS) middleware can be implemented to control access from different origins, useful particularly in RESTful APIs.

```go
func CORSMiddleware(next http.Handler) http.Handler {
  return http.HandlerFunc(func(w http.ResponseWriter, r *http.Request)  { w.Header().Set("Access-Control-Allow-Origin", "*") next.ServeHTTP(w, r)
  })
}
```

Chaining Middleware

One of the powerful features of middleware is the ability to compose multiple middleware functions to apply to a single `http.Handler`. This is typically done by wrapping handlers multiple times, respecting the order in which they are applied.

Here's an example of chaining middleware in a Go web application:

```go
```

```go
func main() {
mux := http.NewServeMux()

mux.HandleFunc("/hello", func(w http.ResponseWriter, r *http.Request) {fmt.Fprintln(w, "Hello, World!")
})
ChainHandler                                    :=
LoggingMiddleware(AuthenticationMiddleware(CORSMi
ddleware(mux)))            http.ListenAndServe(":8080",
ChainHandler)
}
```

In this example, the `http.HandleFunc` is wrapped with three middleware: CORS, Authentication, and Logging. This structure allows for full control over the request lifecycle.

Error Handling in Middleware

Error handling is crucial for web applications to gracefully manage unexpected situations. Middleware can capture errors and respond accordingly.

Here's an example of an error handling middleware:

```go
func       RecoveryMiddleware(next       http.Handler)
http.Handler {
return http.HandlerFunc(func(w http.ResponseWriter, r *http.Request) {defer func() {
if err := recover(); err != nil {
http.Error(w,       "Internal       Server       Error",
```

```
http.StatusInternalServerError) log.Println("Recovered
from error:", err)
}
}()
next.ServeHTTP(w, r)
})
}
```

This middleware uses a deferred function to recover from panics, ensuring that the server does not crash on encountering unexpected errors.

Middleware plays an integral role in Go web applications, offering developers the ability to modularize functionality and enhance overall performance. By applying middleware for tasks like logging, authentication, and error handling, developers can create robust applications that are easier to maintain and extend.

The flexibility of middleware in Go not only promotes code reusability but also allows developers to apply common patterns across different parts of their application. As you continue your Go web development journey, understanding and effectively implementing middleware will be one of the keystones to building resilient and efficient web applications.

Chapter 4: Setting Up Your Go Project Environment

Setting up your Go project environment is a crucial step before diving into programming. A well-structured environment can lead to enhanced productivity, better code management, and a more seamless development experience. In this chapter, we will cover the necessary steps to set up your Go environment, from installation to project structure and the best practices to follow.

4.1 Installing Go

Before you start coding, the first step is to install the Go programming language. Go supports multiple platforms, including Windows, macOS, and Linux. Here's how to get started:

Step 1: Download Go

Visit the official Go website at [golang.org](https://golang.org/dl/) and download the latest version of the Go installer for your operating system. Follow the instructions provided for your specific OS.

Step 2: Install Go

Once the installer is downloaded, run it and follow the installation prompts. The default installation settings are usually sufficient for most users, but you can customize the installation directory if necessary.

Step 3: Verify Installation

After the installation is complete, you need to verify if Go is installed correctly. Open your command line interface (CLI) and run the following command:

```bash
go version
```

You should see the version of Go that you just installed. If you encounter any issues, ensure that the Go binary is included in your system's PATH.

4.2 Setting Up Your Workspace

Go projects are typically organized in a workspace. A workspace is a directory hierarchy with three main subdirectories: `src`, `pkg`, and `bin`.

Step 1: Creating a Workspace

By default, Go looks for your workspace in a directory specified by the `GOPATH` environment variable. To set up your workspace, follow these steps:

Create a directory to hold your workspace. The convention is to use your home directory followed by the `go` label. For example, on macOS/Linux:

```bash
mkdir -p $HOME/go
```

On Windows, you might want to create `C:\Users\YourUsername\go`.

Set the `GOPATH` environment variable to point to this directory. You can usually set this in your shell profile (like `.bashrc`, `.zshrc`, or equivalent). For example:

```bash
export GOPATH=$HOME/go
export PATH=$PATH:$GOPATH/bin
```

After modifying the profile, run `source ~/.bashrc` (or the appropriate command for your shell) to apply the changes.

Step 2: Understanding the Directory Structure
Your workspace will have the following structure:
`src`: Contains Go source files. Each package is stored in its own subdirectory.
`pkg`: Contains compiled package files.
`bin`: Contains compiled binary executables.

Step 3: Creating Your First Go Project
Now that your workspace is set up, it's time to create your first Go project.

Navigate to your `src` directory:

```bash
cd $GOPATH/src
```

Create a new directory for your project, for example, `hello`.

```bash
mkdir hello
cd hello
```

Create a new Go file, `main.go`, and add the following code:

```go
package main
import "fmt"

func main() {
    fmt.Println("Hello, World!")
}
```

Build and run your project by executing:

```bash
go run main.go
```

You should see the output `Hello, World!` printed to your terminal. ## 4.3 Managing Dependencies with Go Modules
With Go 1.11 and later, the introduction of Go modules simplifies the management of dependencies and enables versioning. Here's how to use Go modules in your project:

Step 1: Initializing a Module

In your project directory, initialize a new module by running:

```bash
```

```
go mod init hello
```

This command creates a `go.mod` file that will manage your project's dependencies. ### Step 2: Adding Dependencies
To add a dependency, simply import it in your code, and then run:

```bash
go get github.com/some/dependency
```

This command fetches the dependency and updates your `go.mod` file.### Step 3: Building Your Project
To build your project and all its dependencies, run:

```bash go build
```

This will create an executable file in your project directory.## 4.4 Best Practices for Structuring Your Go Projects
As you grow more comfortable with Go, consider following these best practices when structuring your projects:

Organize Code by Package: Keep related functionality within packages. Create subdirectories in the `src` directory for each package to improve code organization.

Keep Module Small: Aim to create small, focused

modules that only contain code relevant to a specific task. This makes maintenance easier.

Use Meaningful Names: Use descriptive names for your packages, modules, and functions. This will improve code readability and maintainability.

Version Control: Use version control systems like Git to track changes in your code and collaborate with others.

Documentation: Write comments and document your code. Go has built-in support for documentation that can be generated with the `go doc` command.

Test Your Code: Write tests for your code to ensure its functionality and prevent regressions. Go has a built-in testing framework that you can use by creating files ending in `_test.go`.

Setting up your Go project environment is the first step toward productive programming. By installing Go, organizing your workspace, managing dependencies with Go modules, and adhering to best practices, you lay a solid groundwork for your Go development journey. With a properly configured environment, you can focus on writing code that is clean, efficient, and maintainable. In the next chapter, we will dive deeper into the core concepts of the Go language, including its syntax and structure.

Creating and Organizing Go Modules

With the introduction of Go modules in Go 1.11, developers can manage their project dependencies more efficiently and maintain cleaner project structures. This chapter will guide you through creating, organizing, and managing Go modules in your applications. We will cover foundational concepts, practical command usage, best practices, and tips for effective module management.

Understanding Go Modules

Before diving into the creation and organization of Go modules, it's essential to grasp what a Go module is. A Go module is essentially a collection of Go packages that are versioned together. It contains a `go.mod` file, which defines the module's properties, including its name, required dependencies, and their versions.

Key Concepts

Module Path: This is the import path for your module, generally reflecting the repository's location.
Versioning: Go modules support semantic versioning, which facilitates the management of dependencies and allows for predictable updates.
Dependency Resolution: The Go toolchain manages dependencies automatically, ensuring that the correct versions are installed and used during development and runtime.

Creating a Go Module

Creating a Go module is straightforward. Follow these steps to initialize a new module in your Go project: ###

Step 1: Set Up Directory Structure
First, create a new directory for your Go project:

```bash
mkdir myprojectcd myproject
```

Step 2: Initialize the Module

Run the following command to initialize the Go module:

```bash
go mod init github.com/username/myproject
```

Replace `github.com/username/myproject` with your desired module path. This command creates a `go.mod` file in your project directory.

Step 3: Create Go Files

You can start adding Go source files in the same directory. For example, create a file named `main.go`:

```go
package main

import ("fmt"
)

func main() {
fmt.Println("Hello, Go Modules!")
}
```

```
```

Step 4: Manage Dependencies

To add dependencies to your module, you can import the necessary packages in your Go files. When you build or run your module, the Go toolchain will automatically resolve dependencies and add them to the `go.mod` file:

```bash
go run main.go
```

Step 5: Verify Dependencies

After adding dependencies to your project, you can run:

```bash
go mod tidy
```

This command cleans up your `go.mod` file by removing any dependencies that are no longer used and adding missing ones.

Organizing Go Modules

Proper organization of Go modules is critical for maintainability, especially as projects grow in size and complexity. Here are some best practices for organizing your modules.

1. Use Clear and Descriptive Module Names

Select module names that reflect the project's purpose and function. This clarity helps other developers understand the module's role just by looking at its path.

2. Structure Your Codebase Logically

Consider the following directory structure for a project:

``` myproject/go.mod go.sum cmd/
myapp/
main.gopkg/

mypackage1/mypackage2/
internal/ myinternalpackage/
```

`cmd/`: Contains the entry points for your applications.
`pkg/`: Contains library code that can be used by other applications.
`internal/`: Contains packages that are only accessible within the module.### 3. Document Your Code
Use comments and documentation within your code to provide context and clarify the functionality of packages and functions. This practice not only aids your development but also benefits others who may use or contribute to your module.

4. Versioning and Releasing

Utilize Git tags to manage versioning systematically.

Follow semantic versioning (SemVer) to help users understand the significance of updates. This involves:

Major version (X.0.0): Introduces breaking changes.
Minor version (0.Y.0): Adds functionality in a backward-compatible manner.
Patch version (0.0.Z): Introduces backward-compatible bug fixes.To create a new version, use:
```bash
git tag v1.0.0
git push origin v1.0.0
```

5. Continuous Integration/Continuous Deployment (CI/CD)

Integrate CI/CD practices into your workflow to ensure that your modules are tested and deployed efficiently. Use tools like GitHub Actions, Travis CI, or CircleCI to automate testing and deployment.

Creating and organizing Go modules is a fundamental skill for modern Go developers. By following the steps outlined in this chapter, you can set up a robust module structure that promotes clarity, maintainability, and effective dependency management. As you become more familiar with modules, you will find that the Go toolchain provides powerful features that simplify development, testing, and deployment, allowing you to focus on what really matters—building great software.

Managing Dependencies with go.mod

With the introduction of Go Modules, the Go programming language provides a powerful built-in tool designed to simplify the management of dependencies. This chapter explores the `go.mod` file, its structure, and how it can be utilized to manage project dependencies efficiently in the Go ecosystem.

Understanding go.mod

At the heart of the dependency management system in Go lies the `go.mod` file. This file is created in the root directory of a Go module and serves as the primary configuration file for specifying module dependencies. The functionality provided by Go Modules is significant for developers, particularly when dealing with multiple packages or libraries that require specific versions of dependencies.

Creating a go.mod File

To create a new Go module and initialize the `go.mod` file, you can use the following command:

```bash
go mod init <module-name>
```

The `<module-name>` is usually the repository path, such as `github.com/user/repo`. Running this command creates a `go.mod` file that specifies the module's name and initializes it as a module.

Structure of go.mod

The `go.mod` file adopts a simple yet structured syntax. Below is a sample structure of a `go.mod` file:

```go
module github.com/user/repogo 1.18
require (
github.com/gin-gonic/gin                              v1.7.4
google.golang.org/protobuf v1.27.1
)
```

Key Components

Module Declaration: The `module` directive defines the module's name and is usually the import path that users will use to reference it.

Go Version: The `go` directive specifies the semantic version of the Go language that the module is compatible with.

Dependencies: The `require` block lists the external dependencies required by the module, along with their respective versions.

Managing Dependencies

One of the primary functions of the `go.mod` file is to manage the dependencies of your Go module. Below are some of the common commands for managing dependencies:

Adding a Dependency

To add a dependency, you can simply import the package in your Go code. Upon running a build, test, or run command, Go will automatically update the `go.mod` and `go.sum` files to include this new dependency.
Alternatively, you can use:

```bash
go get <package-path>@<version>
```

For example, to add Gin (a popular web framework), you can run:

```bash
go get github.com/gin-gonic/gin
```

This command will pull the latest version of the Gin package, update the `go.mod` file, and also create or update the `go.sum` file to include checksums for the dependencies and their transitive dependencies.

Removing a Dependency

To remove an unused dependency, the simplest way is to delete the relevant import statements from your code and run the following command:

```bash
go mod tidy
```

This command cleans up the `go.mod` file by removing any dependencies that are no longer needed and updates `go.sum` accordingly. Regularly executing `go mod tidy` helps keep your module's dependency list accurate and clean.

Upgrading a Dependency

To upgrade a specific dependency, you can use the following command:

```bash
go get <package-path>@latest
```

This command fetches the latest version of the specified package. If you want a specific version, you can replace `latest` with your desired version number.

Versioning and Semantic Import Versioning

Go Modules employs semantic versioning (SemVer), which is a versioning scheme for determining the stability of releases. This system uses the convention of MAJOR.MINOR.PATCH, where:

MAJOR version changes indicate breaking changes, **MINOR** version changes add functionality in a backward-compatible manner, and
PATCH versions contain backward-compatible bug fixes.

For packages that introduce breaking changes, the Go language encourages the use of semantic import versioning. This means that if a library reaches a new major version (e.g., from v1.x to v2.x), it should be imported with the version reflected in the import path. For instance, you would import a version 2 library as follows:

```go
import "github.com/user/lib/v2"
```

Version Ranges

Go Modules also support version ranges, allowing developers to specify acceptable version ranges for dependencies. While Go does not support specifying version ranges directly in the `go.mod` file like some other package managers, you can use the natural constraints of SemVer. For instance, if you specify that your module requires `github.com/some/library v1.0.0`, Go will resolve to the latest minor and patch versions that are compatible with v1.0.0.

Managing dependencies in Go using the `go.mod` file streamlines the process, making it easier for developers to maintain their projects. By allowing the specification of required modules and their respective versions, Go Modules enhances the stability and reliability of applications. Understanding how to create and manipulate the `go.mod` file is an invaluable skill for Go developers, enabling efficient dependency management as part of their development workflow.

Chapter 5: Designing Modern Web Applications

As we delve into the design principles of modern web applications, this chapter will cover best practices, essential tools, and approaches to create applications that are user-friendly, performant, and maintainable.

5.1 Understanding User-Centric Design

At the heart of any successful web application is the user experience (UX). Designing with the user in mindnot only enhances satisfaction but also drives engagement and conversions. Key principles of user-centric design include:

5.1.1 Research and Personas
Before diving into design, it's crucial to understand your target audience. Conducting user research through surveys, interviews, and usability testing helps you gather insights about user behavior, preferences, and painpoints. From this data, create user personas that represent the different user types interacting with your application. These personas should guide your design decisions throughout the development process.

5.1.2 Usability and Accessibility
Usability ensures that your application is easy to navigate and accomplishes intended tasks without frustration. Incorporating accessibility into your design ensures that your application can be used by individuals with diverse abilities. Employ guidelines such as the Web Content Accessibility Guidelines (WCAG) to create inclusively

designed interfaces.

5.1.3 Interaction Design (IxD)
Interaction design focuses on how users interact with your application. Consider factors like feedback, consistency, and intuitive navigation when designing interactive elements such as buttons, forms, and menus. Creating clear visual hierarchies can guide users through tasks efficiently.

5.2 Architectural Patterns for Scalability and Performance

As web applications become more complex, having a solid architectural foundation is essential. Various architectural patterns serve different needs, particularly concerning scalability, performance, and maintainability.

5.2.1 Single Page Applications (SPAs)
SPAs load a single HTML page and dynamically update content using JavaScript. This approach creates a smoother user experience by reducing reload times and enhancing interactivity. Popular frameworks like React, Angular, and Vue.js are commonly used for SPA development.

5.2.2 Microservices Architecture
Microservices architecture breaks down applications into smaller, independent services that communicate with one another. This approach allows teams to work on different components in parallel, scaling parts of the application as needed. It's suitable for larger applications that require flexibility and rapid deployment.

5.2.3 Progressive Web Apps (PWAs)
PWAs blend the best of web and mobile applications, offering features such as offline access, push notifications, and app-like user experiences. They leverage modern web capabilities for performance and can be installed on devices, ensuring a seamless user experience across platforms.

5.3 Choosing the Right Tech Stack

Selecting the appropriate tech stack is vital for the success of your web application. Your choice can affect performance, scalability, and maintainability.

5.3.1 Frontend Technologies
The frontend is where users interact with your application. Choose a framework that aligns with your project requirements. Frameworks such as React, Vue.js, and Angular offer different strengths in speed, versatility, and community support. Additionally, adopting CSS preprocessors (e.g., SASS, LESS) and UI libraries (e.g., Bootstrap, Material-UI) can enhance the visual appeal and responsiveness of your application.

5.3.2 Backend Technologies
The backend handles data storage, processing, and business logic. Common options include Node.js for JavaScript-based development, Django for Python enthusiasts, Ruby on Rails, and .NET for enterprise solutions. Consider your team's skill set and the specific requirements of your application when choosing a backend framework.

5.3.3 Databases and APIs
Data persistence is key in web applications. Relational databases (e.g., PostgreSQL, MySQL) and NoSQL databases (e.g., MongoDB) serve different data storage needs. When integrating third-party services, RESTful APIs and GraphQL are popular approaches, offering flexibility in data retrieval.

5.4 Responsive and Adaptive Design

The proliferation of devices with varying screen sizes necessitates that modern web applications be both responsive and adaptive. Responsive design employs fluid grids, flexible images, and media queries, ensuring that your application functions optimally across a range of devices. Adaptive design, on the other hand, involves designing distinct layouts for different screen sizes.

5.4.1 Mobile-First Approach
Designing with mobile users in mind first—before scaling up to larger screens—ensures that the core functionality is preserved across devices. This approach prioritizes speed, simplicity, and essential content, which contributes to a superior user experience.

5.5 Testing and Quality Assurance

Continuous testing is integral to developing a reliable web application. Implement a comprehensive testing strategy that includes:

5.5.1 Unit Testing

Ensure individual components function correctly through unit testing. Frameworks like Jest (for JavaScript) or JUnit (for Java) can be employed to validate logic at the code level.

5.5.2 Integration Testing
Post integration testing verifies that different components of your application interact as intended. This stage helps identify any issues arising from combined components.

5.5.3 User Acceptance Testing (UAT)
Gather feedback from real users to validate that the application meets their needs and expectations. UAT plays a crucial role in refining the application before its final launch.

By adhering to best practices in user-centric design, choosing the right tech stack, and employing thorough testing methods, developers can create applications that not only meet user requirements but also stand the test of time. As we continue to explore the evolving web landscape, the principles discussed in this chapter will be essential tools in your web development arsenal.

Structuring Code and Application Layers

The way we designate responsibilities among various parts of an application not only influences the maintainability and scalability of the software but also impacts the ease of collaboration among development teams. This chapter explores the key principles and best practices for structuring code and layers within modern application architectures.

1. Understanding Application Layers ### 1.1 What Are Application Layers?

Application layers refer to the distinct levels of abstraction in a software system where specific functionalities and responsibilities are allocated. The most common layers include:

Presentation Layer: This is the user interface layer that interacts with the end-user. It is responsible for displaying information and handling user input. In web applications, this could manifest as HTML, CSS, and JavaScript.

Business Logic Layer (BLL): This layer contains the core functionality of the application — the logic that dictates how data can be created, stored, and changed. It serves as a bridge between the user interface and the data, processing user inputs and returning necessary outputs.

Data Access Layer (DAL): This layer is responsible for interacting with the data storage mechanism, whether it be a database, file system, or external services. It performs CRUD (Create, Read, Update, Delete) operations and abstracts the details of the data source from other layers.

1.2 Benefits of Layered Architecture

A layered architecture provides several advantages:

Separation of Concerns: Each layer has a distinct responsibility, making it easier to manage and understand the system. Developers can focus on specific layers without the overhead of dealing with the entire system.

Reusability: By structuring code into layers, components can be reused across different applications or different parts of the same application. For instance, the same business logic can potentially serve multiple interfaces.

Maintainability: Changes in one layer can often be made without significantly impacting other layers. For example, updating the presentation layer technology might not require changes in the underlying business or data layers.

Easy Testing: Layered architecture enables more straightforward testing since layers can be tested independently. Unit tests can focus on the BLL without concern for how data is presented or stored.

2. Principles of Structuring Code

2.1 Follow Established Design Patterns

Utilizing established design patterns is key to maintaining a structured codebase. Common patterns include:

MVC (Model-View-Controller): A popular architecture model that separates an application into three interconnected components, allowing for efficient code management.

MVVM (Model-View-ViewModel): Particularly useful in UI-heavy applications, it separates the development of the graphical user interface from the business logic.

Repository Pattern: This pattern promotes a clean separation between the data access layer and the business logic, enhancing testing and scalability.

2.2 Keep Code DRY (Don't Repeat Yourself)

Repetition in code leads to increased maintenance costs and bugs. By following the DRY principle, developers should encapsulate common functionality into reusable components or functions, minimizing duplication and fostering a more organized structure.

2.3 Use Meaningful Naming Conventions

Readable code is more maintainable code. Consistent and meaningful naming conventions provide clarity regarding each component's purpose, aiding teamwork and collaboration. Classes, methods, and variables should clearly convey their roles within the application.

2.4 Modularize Your Code

Breaking down functionality into smaller, reusable modules allows for greater maintainability. Each module should encapsulate a specific set of behaviors or responsibilities, fostering clearer organization and making it easier to identify and fix bugs.

3. Organizing Code within Layers

3.1 Structuring the Presentation Layer

Component-Based Architecture: Adopt a component-based approach to the presentation layer, where UI components are self-contained and reusable. Tools like React, Angular, and Vue.js facilitate this structure.

Responsive Design: Implement responsive design to ensure that applications function well across various devices and screen sizes without duplicating code.

3.2 Structuring the Business Logic Layer

Service-Oriented Architecture: Create services that embody specific business functions. This not only promotes reusability but also aligns well with microservices architectures, where individual services can scale independently.

Error Handling: Implement centralized error handling strategies to manage exceptions effectively across the business layer, providing a consistent user experience.

3.3 Structuring the Data Access Layer

Data Models: Use data models to define the structure of the data and its relationships, allowing for easier database changes and migrations.

Database Abstraction: Introducing an abstraction layer over your database can facilitate database swapping or migration without resulting in extensive code changes.

By adhering to established principles and design patterns,

developers can create robust and organized applications that stand the test of time. As we continue to advance in technology and methodologies, the importance of thoughtful structure in code remains paramount in building applications that not only fulfill functional requirements but also deliver a great user experience. Understanding and implementing these concepts pave the way for the development of high-quality software that meets the demands of the modern digital landscape.

Handling Routes and URL Patterns in Go

In Go, often referred to as Golang, the built-in `net/http` package provides a simple way to handle routing. However, for more complex applications, developers often utilize third-party libraries to enhance routing capabilities. In this chapter, we will explore basic routing concepts in Go and introduce some popular libraries that can simplify the handling of routes and URL patterns.

Understanding the Basics of Routing

Routing is the mechanism that determines how an application responds to a client request for a particular resource. In Go, routing is primarily managed through the HTTP server, which utilizes the `http.ServeMux` type, a type specifically designed to serve HTTP requests.

Creating a Simple HTTP Server

To illustrate routing, let's start by creating a simple HTTP server in Go that handles a few basic routes. This example will demonstrate how you can map URLs to specific handler functions.

```go
package main

import ( "fmt" "net/http"
)

// Handler for the root route
func    homeHandler(w    http.ResponseWriter,    r
*http.Request) { fmt.Fprintf(w, "Welcome to the Home
Page!")
}

// Handler for the About route
func    aboutHandler(w    http.ResponseWriter,    r
*http.Request) {fmt.Fprintf(w, "This is the About Page.")
}

// Main function to start the serverfunc main() {
// Create a new ServeMux mux := http.NewServeMux()

// Register route handlers mux.HandleFunc("/",
homeHandler) mux.HandleFunc("/about", aboutHandler)

// Start the server http.ListenAndServe(":8080", mux)
}
```

In this example, we register two routes: the root route ("/") and the "/about" route. Each route is linked to a corresponding handler function that processes the request and generates a response.

Understanding URL Patterns

In addition to static routes, Go's routing can handle URL patterns that may include path parameters. For instance, if we wanted to create a profile route that captures a user ID, we could employ string manipulation techniques to extract parameters from the URL.

Handling Dynamic URL Patterns

```go
package main

import ( "fmt" "net/http""strings"
)

// Handler for dynamic user profile route
func        profileHandler(w        http.ResponseWriter,        r
*http.Request) {
// Extract the user ID from the URL parts :=
strings.Split(r.URL.Path, "/")iflen(parts) < 3 {
http.Error(w,        "User        ID        is        required",
http.StatusBadRequest)return
}
userID := parts[2]
fmt.Fprintf(w, "Profile Page of User: %s", userID)
}
```

```
func main() {
mux := http.NewServeMux()

mux.HandleFunc("/",                          homeHandler)
mux.HandleFunc("/about", aboutHandler)
mux.HandleFunc("/profile/", profileHandler) // Notice
the trailing slash

http.ListenAndServe(":8080", mux)
}
```

In the code snippet above, we created a `profileHandler`
that processes requests to a dynamic route. The handler
expects the URL to contain a user ID after the `/profile/`
segment. We extract the user ID by splitting the URL path.

Utilizing Third-Party Routing Libraries

While Go's built-in routing capabilities provide a solid
foundation, using a third-party router can greatly enhance
your application's organization and readability, especially
as it grows in complexity. Here, we will discuss some
popular routing libraries available in the Go ecosystem.

1. Gorilla Mux

One of the most commonly used packages for routing in
Go is `Gorilla Mux`. It provides powerful routing features,
including regular expression matching, route variables,
and more.

Installation

To use Gorilla Mux, you can install it via Go modules:

```bash
go get -u github.com/gorilla/mux
```

Example Usage

Here's how you can use Gorilla Mux to build a similar application with more advanced routing capabilities:

```go
package main

import ( "fmt" "net/http"
"github.com/gorilla/mux"
)

func main() {
r := mux.NewRouter()

r.HandleFunc("/", homeHandler) r.HandleFunc("/about",
aboutHandler)
r.HandleFunc("/profile/{userid}",    profileHandler)    //
Route variable

http.ListenAndServe(":8080", r)
}

func    profileHandler(w    http.ResponseWriter,    r
*http.Request) {vars := mux.Vars(r)
userID := vars["userid"]
```

```
fmt.Fprintf(w, "Profile Page of User: %s", userID)
}
```

In this example, we define a route that captures the user ID using the `{userid}` syntax. The `mux.Vars` function allows us to easily retrieve the variable from the request.

2. Chi

Another minimalist and performant router for Go is Chi. It is lightweight and built on the principles of simplicity and performance.

Installation

You can install Chi as follows:

```bash
go get -u github.com/go-chi/chi/v5
```

Example Usage

Here's a simple example using Chi:

```go
package main

import ( "fmt" "net/http"
"github.com/go-chi/chi/v5"
)
```

```go
func main() {
r := chi.NewRouter()

r.Get("/", homeHandler) r.Get("/about", aboutHandler)
r.Get("/profile/{userid}", profileHandler) // Route
variable

http.ListenAndServe(":8080", r)
}

func profileHandler(w http.ResponseWriter, r
*http.Request) {userID := chi.URLParam(r, "userid")
fmt.Fprintf(w, "Profile Page of User: %s", userID)
}
```

Much like Gorilla Mux, Chi simplifies route management and provides easy access to route parameters.

Handling routes and URL patterns in Go is essential for developing web applications that respond to user inputs effectively. The built-in `net/http` package offers a solid foundation for routing basics, allowing developers to create simple server applications. However, as applications grow in complexity, utilizing third- party libraries like Gorilla Mux or Chi offers enhanced routing capabilities, simplicity, and flexibility.

Chapter 6: Integrating Relational Databases with Go

Relational databases provide a reliable way to store, manage, and retrieve structured data. This chapter will explore the integration of relational databases into Go applications, focusing on connection management, CRUD operations, and best practices to ensure your application remains robust and efficient.

6.1 Understanding Relational Databases

Relational databases store data in tables, rows, and columns. Each table represents a different entity, and relationships between tables can be established using foreign keys. Popular relational databases include MySQL, PostgreSQL, SQLite, and MariaDB. Each database has its unique features, but the underlying principles of SQL (Structured Query Language) remain mostly the same.

In this chapter, we will primarily use PostgreSQL as our primary example, though the principles can easily extend to other relational databases.

6.2 Setting Up Your Environment

Before diving into coding, you'll need to ensure that you have a PostgreSQL instance running. You can install it locally or use a cloud-based service for development. Follow these steps to set up your environment:

Install PostgreSQL: Download and install PostgreSQL from the [official

website](https://www.postgresql.org/download/).
Create a Database: After installation, create a new database where you'll store your data. You can use the `psql` command-line utility or a graphical tool like pgAdmin.
Install Go: Make sure you have Go installed on your machine. If not, download it from the [official Go website](https://golang.org/dl/).

6.3 Connecting to the Database

To connect to a PostgreSQL database in Go, we'll use the `pq` package, which is a pure Go driver for PostgreSQL. You can install it with the following command:

```bash
go get -u github.com/lib/pq
```

Here's how you can connect to the database:

```go
package main

import ( "database/sql""fmt"
"log"
```

```go
    _ "github.com/lib/pq"
)

func main() {
connStr := "user=yourusername dbname=yourdbname
password=yourpassword sslmode=disable" db, err :=
sql.Open("postgres", connStr)
if err != nil { log.Fatal(err)
}
defer db.Close()

err = db.Ping()if err != nil {
log.Fatal("Cannot connect to the database:", err)
}

fmt.Println("Successfully connected to the database!")
}
```

Connection String Parameters

user: The database username.
dbname: The name of the database.
password: The password for the specified user.
sslmode: Use `disable` during development, but
consider changing this to `require` in production for
security reasons.

6.4 CRUD Operations

CRUD stands for Create, Read, Update, and Delete—
functions that correspond to the basic operations you'll
perform on your database.

6.4.1 Creating Records

To add records to your database, you can use the `INSERT` SQL statement. Here's an example of how to create a new entry in a `users` table:

```go
func createUser(db *sql.DB, name string, age int) {
sqlStatement := `INSERT INTO users (name, age) VALUES ($1, $2) RETURNING id`id := 0
err := db.QueryRow(sqlStatement, name, age).Scan(&id)if err != nil {
log.Fatalf("Unable to insert user: %v", err)
}
fmt.Printf("User created with ID: %d\n", id)
}
```

6.4.2 Reading Records

To retrieve data from the database, you can use the `SELECT` statement. Here's how to fetch all users:

```go
func getUsers(db *sql.DB) {
rows, err := db.Query("SELECT id, name, age FROM users")if err != nil {
log.Fatal(err)
}
defer rows.Close()

for rows.Next() {var id int
```

```go
var name stringvar age int
err := rows.Scan(&id, &name, &age)if err != nil {
log.Fatal(err)
}
fmt.Printf("ID: %d, Name: %s, Age: %d\n", id, name, age)
}
}
```

6.4.3 Updating Records

To update existing records, use the `UPDATE` SQL
statement. Here's an example of how to update a user's
age:

```go
func updateUserAge(db *sql.DB, id int, newAge int) {
sqlStatement := `UPDATE users SET age=$1 WHERE
id=$2`
_, err := db.Exec(sqlStatement, newAge, id)if err != nil {
log.Fatalf("Unable to update user: %v", err)
}
fmt.Printf("User with ID: %d updated to age: %d\n", id,
newAge)
}
```

6.4.4 Deleting Records

To delete a record, you can use the `DELETE` SQL
statement. Here's how to remove a user from thedatabase:

```go
```

```go
func deleteUser(db *sql.DB, id int) {
sqlStatement := `DELETE FROM users WHERE id=$1`
_, err := db.Exec(sqlStatement, id)if err != nil {
log.Fatalf("Unable to delete user: %v", err)
}
fmt.Printf("User with ID: %d deleted\n", id)
}
```

6.5 Error Handling and Transactions

When dealing with databases, error handling is crucial. Always check for errors after executing any SQL command. Furthermore, you should consider using transactions to ensure data integrity when executing multiple related operations.

Here's an example of how to use transactions in Go:

```go
func updateUser(db *sql.DB, id int, name string, age int) {
tx, err := db.Begin()
if err != nil { log.Fatal(err)
}

_, err = tx.Exec(`UPDATE users SET name=$1, age=$2 WHERE id=$3`, name, age, id)if err != nil {
tx.Rollback()log.Fatal(err)
}

err = tx.Commit()if err != nil {
log.Fatal(err)
}
```

```
fmt.Printf("User with ID: %d updated successfully\n", id)
}
```

6.6 Best Practices

Use Prepared Statements: Always use prepared statements to avoid SQL injection vulnerabilities.
Handle Errors Properly: Log errors and handle them appropriately to ensure your application can recover gracefully.
Connection Pooling: Use connection pooling to improve performance, especially under heavy load.
Close Connections: Always close your database connections to prevent resource leaks.
Migrations: Use a migration tool (like `golang-migrate`) to manage database schema changes.

By mastering the art of CRUD operations and following best practices, you can ensure your application isreliable, maintainable, and secure. In the next chapter, we will explore advanced database features such as indexing, foreign keys, and joins, further enhancing your ability to work with relational databases in Go.

Connecting to SQL Databases in GO

This chapter will walk you through the process of connecting to SQL databases in Go, using the `database/sql` package alongside various database drivers. We will cover the following topics:

Installing the necessary packages
Configuring the database connection
Performing basic CRUD operations
Handling errors and closing connections ## 1. Installing Necessary Packages
Before we start coding, make sure you have Go installed on your system. You can download it from the official [Go website](https://golang.org/). Once Go is set up, you need to install the relevant SQL driver for the database you want to connect to.

For instance, if you want to connect to a PostgreSQL database, you will need to install the `pgx` driver, which is widely used in the Go community. You can install it using the `go get` command:

```bash
go get github.com/jackc/pgx/v4
```

For connecting to MySQL, you would use:

```bash
go get github.com/go-sql-driver/mysql
```

For SQLite, you can install:

```bash
go get github.com/mattn/go-sqlite3
```

Make sure to choose and install the driver that

corresponds to the database you intend to use. ## 2. Configuring the Database Connection

With the necessary packages installed, you can now set up a connection to your SQL database. For this example, we will create a simple Go application that connects to a PostgreSQL database.

First, create a new Go file called `main.go` and add the following code:

```go
package main

import (
"context" "database/sql""fmt"

"log"

"github.com/jackc/pgx/v4/pgxpool"
)

func main() {
dsn := "user=username password=yourpassword dbname=yourdb host=localhost sslmode=disable"dbpool,
err := pgxpool.Connect(context.Background(), dsn)
if err != nil {
log.Fatalf("Unable to connect to database: %v", err)


}
```

```
}
defer dbpool.Close()

fmt.Println("Successfully connected to the database!")
```

Breakdown of the Code

Importing Packages: We import the necessary packages, including the PostgreSQL driver and context for managing the connection lifecycle.
Data Source Name (DSN): A DSN string is constructed to provide connection parameters such as username, password, database name, host, and SSL mode.
Establishing Connection: We use `pgxpool.Connect()` to connect to the database, which provides a connection pool for better resource management.
Error Handling: It's crucial to handle errors during connection establishment to prevent runtime crashes.
Deferred Close: The `dbpool.Close()` function is deferred to ensure that the connection pool is closed when the main function exits.

3. Performing Basic CRUD Operations

Once you have established a connection to the database, you can perform SQL queries. Let's implement basic CRUD (Create, Read, Update, Delete) operations.

Create Operation

To insert a record into your database, you can use the

following code snippet:

```go
func createUser(dbpool *pgxpool.Pool, name string, age
int) error {
_, err := dbpool.Exec(context.Background(), "INSERT
INTO users(name, age) VALUES($1, $2)", name,age)
return err
}
```

Read Operation

To read records, use a query and scan the results:

```go
func getUsers(dbpool *pgxpool.Pool) {
rows,    err    :=    dbpool.Query(context.Background(),
"SELECT id, name, age FROM users")

if err != nil {
log.Fatalf("Query failed: %v", err)
}
defer rows.Close()

for rows.Next() {var id int
var name stringvar age int
if err := rows.Scan(&id, &name, &age); err != nil {
log.Fatalf("Scan failed: %v", err)



}
```

```
    }
```}
fmt.Printf("User: %d, Name: %s, Age: %d\n", id, name, age)

Update Operation

To update a record, use the following function:

```go
func updateUserAge(dbpool *pgxpool.Pool, id int, newAge int) error {
_, err := dbpool.Exec(context.Background(), "UPDATE users SET age=$1 WHERE id=$2", newAge, id)return err
}
```


Delete Operation Finally, to delete a user:
```go
func deleteUser(dbpool *pgxpool.Pool, id int) error {
_, err := dbpool.Exec(context.Background(), "DELETE FROM users WHERE id=$1", id)return err
}
```


Putting It All Together

You can call these functions in your `main()` function:

```go
func main() {
// ... connection code ...
```

```go
// Create a new user
if err := createUser(dbpool, "John Doe", 30); err != nil {
log.Fatalf("Insert failed: %v", err)
}

// Get and display usersgetUsers(dbpool)

// Update user age
if err := updateUserAge(dbpool, 1, 31); err != nil {
log.Fatalf("Update failed: %v", err)
}

// Delete user
if err := deleteUser(dbpool, 1); err != nil {
log.Fatalf("Delete failed: %v", err)
}
}
```

4. Handling Errors and Closing Connections

When dealing with database operations, it's essential to handle errors gracefully and ensure that connectionsare properly closed. Go encourages the use of error handling through explicit checks, which we have implemented throughout the CRUD operations. By utilizing `defer`, we ensure that resources are released correctly when they are no longer needed.

Connecting to SQL databases in Go is a straightforward process that involves setting up the appropriate packages, constructing a connection string, and implementing

various operations to manipulate data. The
`database/sql` package offers a powerful and flexible way
to interact with different SQL databases, making it
versatile for various applications. With Go's concurrent
capabilities and efficient performance, working with
databases becomes a seamless component of your
development workflow.

Performing CRUD Operations in Go

In this chapter, we'll explore how to perform CRUD
operations using Go, a statically typed, compiledlanguage
that has gained popularity for its simplicity and efficiency.

Setting Up the Environment

Before diving into CRUD operations, ensure Go is
installed on your machine. You can download it from the
official Go website and follow the installation instructions.
After installing Go, set up a new project directory:

```bash
mkdir go-crud-examplecd go-crud-example
go mod init go-crud-example
```

Choosing a Database

For this chapter, we will use SQLite for its lightweight
nature, which makes it straightforward for
demonstrations and testing. SQLite comes as a single
library that requires no server setup. To interact with

SQLite in Go, we will use the `github.com/mattn/go-sqlite3` package.

First, you need to install the SQLite driver:

```bash
go get -u github.com/mattn/go-sqlite3
```

Project Structure

The project structure for our CRUD application will be simple:

```
go-crud-example/main.go
db/
database.gomodels/
user.go
```

1. Defining the User Model

Create a `user.go` file in the `models` directory with the following content:

```go
package models

type User struct {
ID     int     `json:"id"`

Name string `json:"name"`Email string `json:"email"`
```

```
}
```

This struct defines our `User` model with three fields: `ID`, `Name`, and `Email`. ### 2. Setting Up the Database

In the `db` directory, create `database.go` which will handle all database operations:

```go
package db

import ( "database/sql""log"
"github.com/mattn/go-sqlite3"              "go-crud-
example/models"
)
var Db *sql.DBfunc Init() {
var err error
Db, err = sql.Open("sqlite3", "./users.db")if err != nil {
log.Fatal(err)
}

createTableQuery := `CREATE TABLE IF NOT EXISTS
users (id INTEGER PRIMARY KEY AUTOINCREMENT,
name TEXT,email TEXT
);`

if _, err := Db.Exec(createTableQuery); err != nil {
log.Fatal(err)
}
}
```

In this file:

We initialize a SQLite database connection.
We create a `users` table if it doesn't already exist. This table will store user records.### 3. Implementing CRUD Operations
Next, implement the CRUD functions in `database.go`:

```go
// CreateUser inserts a new user into the database func CreateUser(user models.User) (int64, error) {
stmt, err := Db.Prepare("INSERT INTO users(name, email) VALUES(?, ?)")

if err != nil { return 0, err
}
defer stmt.Close()

res, err := stmt.Exec(user.Name, user.Email)if err != nil {
return 0, err
}

return res.LastInsertId()
}

// GetUser retrieves a user by ID
func GetUser(id int) (models.User, error) { var user models.User
err := Db.QueryRow("SELECT id, name, email FROM users WHERE id = ?", id).Scan(&user.ID, &user.Name, &user.Email)
if err != nil { return user, err
}
return user, nil
}
```

```go
// UpdateUser modifies an existing user's information
func UpdateUser(user models.User) error {
stmt, err := Db.Prepare("UPDATE users SET name = ?,
email = ? WHERE id = ?")if err != nil {
return err
}
defer stmt.Close()

_, err = stmt.Exec(user.Name, user.Email, user.ID)return
err
}

// DeleteUser removes a user from the database func
DeleteUser(id int) error {
stmt, err := Db.Prepare("DELETE FROM users WHERE
id = ?")if err != nil {
return err
}
defer stmt.Close()

_, err = stmt.Exec(id)return err
}
```

4. Creating the Main Application

Now, create the `main.go` file to bring everything together:

```go
package main
```

```go
import ( "encoding/json""net/http" "strconv"
"github.com/gorilla/mux""go-crud-example/db"
"go-crud-example/models"
)

func main() {db.Init()
router := mux.NewRouter()

router.HandleFunc("/users",
CreateUserHandler).Methods("POST")
router.HandleFunc("/users/{id}",
GetUserHandler).Methods("GET")
router.HandleFunc("/users/{id}",
UpdateUserHandler).Methods("PUT")
router.HandleFunc("/users/{id}",
DeleteUserHandler).Methods("DELETE")

http.ListenAndServe(":8000", router)
}

// CreateUserHandler handles POST requests to create a
new       user       func       CreateUserHandler(w
http.ResponseWriter, r *http.Request) {
var                user                models.User
json.NewDecoder(r.Body).Decode(&user) id,  err  :=
db.CreateUser(user)
if err != nil {
http.Error(w, err.Error(), http.StatusInternalServerError)
return
}
w.WriteHeader(http.StatusCreated)
json.NewEncoder(w).Encode(map[string]int64{"id": id})
}
```

```go
// GetUserHandler handles GET requests to retrieve a
user
func GetUserHandler(w http.ResponseWriter, r
*http.Request) {params := mux.Vars(r)
id, _ := strconv.Atoi(params["id"]) user, err :=
db.GetUser(id)
if err != nil {
http.Error(w, err.Error(), http.StatusNotFound)return
}
json.NewEncoder(w).Encode(user)
}

// UpdateUserHandler handles PUT requests to update
user information func UpdateUserHandler(w
http.ResponseWriter, r *http.Request) {
params := mux.Vars(r)
id, _ := strconv.Atoi(params["id"])

var user models.User
json.NewDecoder(r.Body).Decode(&user)user.ID = id
if err := db.UpdateUser(user); err != nil {
http.Error(w, err.Error(), http.StatusInternalServerError)
return
}
w.WriteHeader(http.StatusNoContent)
}

// DeleteUserHandler handles DELETE requests to
remove a user func DeleteUserHandler(w
http.ResponseWriter, r *http.Request) {
params := mux.Vars(r)
id, _ := strconv.Atoi(params["id"])
```

```go
if err := db.DeleteUser(id); err != nil { http.Error(w,
err.Error(), http.StatusNotFound)
}
w.WriteHeader(http.StatusNoContent)
}
```

5. Testing the CRUD API

To test the functionality of our CRUD API, you can use tools like Postman or cURL. Here are some basic commands to test your API endpoints:

Create a User:

```bash
curl -X POST -H "Content-Type: application/json" -d
'{"name":"John Doe", "email":"john@example.com"}'
http://localhost:8000/users
```

Get User By ID:

```bash
curl http://localhost:8000/users/1
```

Update User:

```bash
curl -X PUT -H "Content-Type: application/json" -d
'{"name":"John                            Smith",
"email":"johnsmith@example.com"}'
```

http://localhost:8000/users/1
```

**Delete User**:

```bash
curl -X DELETE http://localhost:8000/users/1
```

In this chapter, we have built a simple CRUD API in Go utilizing SQLite as our database. We created a structure to manage user data, implemented create, read, update, and delete operations, and set up a RESTful API to interact with our user data.
```

Chapter 7: Leveraging NoSQL Databases in GoApplications

This chapter delves into how to effectively integrate NoSQL databases with Go applications, exploring the paradigms, best practices, and potential libraries you can use to facilitate development. We will also cover common NoSQL databases, including MongoDB, Couchbase, and Redis, highlighting their features and howthey align with Go's strengths.

7.1 Understanding NoSQL Databases

Before diving into implementation, it's essential to understand the core characteristics that differentiate NoSQL databases from traditional relational databases. NoSQL databases prioritize:

Schema Flexibility: NoSQL databases typically allow for a dynamic schema, enabling developers tostore data in a more flexible format. This is particularly useful for applications where data structures evolveover time.

Horizontal Scalability: Unlike traditional databases, which often require vertical scaling, many NoSQL databases are designed to scale out by adding more servers. This is crucial for applications thathandle large volumes of data and concurrent users.

High Availability and Performance: Many NoSQL systems are designed to provide high availabilityand low latency, making them ideal for real-time applications.

Data Models: NoSQL databases come in several types, including document stores, key-value stores, wide-column stores, and graph databases, each suited for different use cases.

7.2 Choosing the Right NoSQL Database

Selecting the appropriate NoSQL database for your Go application largely depends on your specific use case:

MongoDB: A popular document store that is easy to use and integrates seamlessly with Go through various libraries. Ideal for applications that deal with semi-structured data.

Redis: A key-value store known for its exceptional speed and support for complex data types. It's great for caching, session management, and real-time analytics.

Couchbase: Combines the capabilities of key-value stores with the query features of document databases. It's suitable for applications requiring high availability and scalability.

Cassandra: A wide-column store designed for high availability across multiple data centers. It's ideal for applications needing linear scalability with minimal downtime.

7.3 Setting Up MongoDB with Go

In this section, we will explore how to set up and interact with MongoDB using the official Go driver. Here are the steps to get started.

7.3.1 Installation

To manage MongoDB in a Go application, you first need to install the MongoDB Go driver:

```bash
go get go.mongodb.org/mongo-driver/mongo
```

7.3.2 Connecting to MongoDB

Here's how you can connect to a MongoDB instance in your Go application:

```go
package main

import ( "context""fmt"
"go.mongodb.org/mongo-driver/mongo"
"go.mongodb.org/mongo-driver/mongo/options""log"
)

func main() {
clientOptions                                  :=
options.Client().ApplyURI("mongodb://localhost:27017")
client,    err    :=    mongo.Connect(context.TODO(),
clientOptions)

if err != nil { log.Fatal(err)
}
```

```go
err = client.Ping(context.TODO(), nil)if err != nil {
log.Fatal(err)
}

fmt.Println("Connected to MongoDB!")
}
```

7.3.3 Performing CRUD Operations

Now let's look at how to perform basic CRUD (Create, Read, Update, Delete) operations: #### Create
```go
collection := client.Database("testdb").Collection("users")
user := bson.D{{"name", "John Doe"}, {"age", 30}}

insertResult, err := collection.InsertOne(context.TODO(), user)if err != nil {
log.Fatal(err)
}
fmt.Println("Inserted a single document: ", insertResult.InsertedID)
```

Read

```go
var result bson.M
err = collection.FindOne(context.TODO(), bson.D{{"name", "John Doe"}}).Decode(&result)if err != nil {
log.Fatal(err)
}
```

```go
fmt.Println("Found a single document: ", result)
```

Update

```go
filter := bson.D{{"name", "John Doe"}}
update := bson.D{{"$set", bson.D{{"age", 31}}}}

_, err = collection.UpdateOne(context.TODO(), filter, update)if err != nil {
log.Fatal(err)
}
fmt.Println("Updated a single document")
```

Delete

```go
_, err = collection.DeleteOne(context.TODO(), bson.D{{"name", "John Doe"}})if err != nil {
log.Fatal(err)
}
fmt.Println("Deleted a single document")
```

7.4 Leveraging Redis for Caching and More

Redis can be utilized to significantly improve the performance of your Go application by caching frequently accessed data. Its in-memory architecture allows for fast read and write operations.

7.4.1 Installation

To integrate Redis, you can use the go-redis client:

```bash
go get github.com/go-redis/redis/v8
```

7.4.2 Using Redis for Caching

Here's a sample implementation of retrieving and caching data with Redis:

```go
package main

import ( "context""fmt"
"github.com/go-redis/redis/v8""log"
)
var ctx = context.Background()func main() {
rdb    :=    redis.NewClient(&redis.Options{    Addr:
"localhost:6379",
})

// Cache example
err := rdb.Set(ctx, "mykey", "hello world", 0).Err()if err !=
nil {
log.Fatalf("Could not set key: %v", err)
}

val, err := rdb.Get(ctx, "mykey").Result()if err != nil {
log.Fatalf("Could not get key: %v", err)
}
```

```
fmt.Println("Value of 'mykey':", val)
}
```

7.5 Best Practices for Using NoSQL with Go

Data Modeling: Plan your data model according to the specific features of the NoSQL database you choose. Understand how to store and retrieve related data effectively.

Error Handling: Given the asynchronous nature of many NoSQL operations, ensure robust error handling in your code.

Connection Management: Use connection pooling to manage database connections efficiently, particularly under load.

Monitoring and Logging: Leverage monitoring tools to track database performance and errors. Logging is essential for debugging and maintaining your application.

Documentation: Always refer to the official documentation for the database you are working with to understand best practices, configuration options, and limitations.

Integrating NoSQL databases into your Go applications can provide significant benefits regarding scalability, flexibility, and performance. By choosing the right database for your specific needs and following best practices for implementation, you can unlock the true potential of your application.

Setting Up MongoDB in Go

When paired with the Go programming language, which is renowned for its performance and simplicity, you can build efficient and scalable applications that leverage the strengths of both tools. This chapter will guide you through the process of setting up MongoDB in a Go environment, from installation to basic CRUD operations.

Prerequisites

Before we dive into the setup process, ensure you have the following installed on your machine:

Go: Download and install the latest version of Go from the [official site](https://golang.org/dl/).
MongoDB: Install MongoDB by following the instructions on the [MongoDB installation page](https://docs.mongodb.com/manual/installation/).
Go MongoDB Driver: We will use the official MongoDB driver for Go, which can be installed via Go modules.

Step 1: Installing MongoDB ### On macOS
If you're on macOS, you can easily install MongoDB using Homebrew:

```bash
brew tap mongodb/brew
brew install mongodb-community
```

```
```

On Windows

For Windows, you can download the MongoDB MSI installer from the [MongoDB download center](https://www.mongodb.com/try/download/community) and follow the installation instructions provided there.

On Linux

For Linux distributions, refer to the [MongoDB installation guide](https://docs.mongodb.com/manual/administration/install-on-linux/) for detailed steps appropriate for your distribution.

Starting the MongoDB Service

Once MongoDB is installed, you can start the server. Use the following command in your terminal:

```bash mongod
```

This command starts the MongoDB server process. If you wish to run it as a service, look into the appropriate service management commands for your operating system.

Step 2: Install the Go MongoDB Driver

You can use the official MongoDB driver for Go to interact with your MongoDB database. To install it, open your terminal and navigate to your Go project directory. Then run:

```bash
go get go.mongodb.org/mongo-driver/mongo
```

This command fetches the MongoDB driver and adds it to your project.## Step 3: Building a Simple Application
Now that you have MongoDB and the Go driver set up, let's create a simple application that performs basic CRUD (Create, Read, Update, Delete) operations.

Step 3.1: Initialize Your Go Project

Create a new directory for your Go project and change into it. Then initialize a new Go module:

```bash
mkdir go-mongodb-examplecd go-mongodb-example
go mod init go-mongodb-example
```

Step 3.2: Create a MongoDB Client Next, create a main.go file:
```go
package main

import (
"context""fmt"
"log"
```

```go
    "time"

    "go.mongodb.org/mongo-driver/mongo"
    "go.mongodb.org/mongo-driver/mongo/options"
)

func main() {
    // Set client options and connect to MongoDB
    clientOptions                                        :=
options.Client().ApplyURI("mongodb://localhost:27017")

    // Create a new client and connect to the server
    client,       err       :=       mongo.Connect(context.TODO(),
clientOptions)if err != nil {
    log.Fatal(err)
    }

    // Check the connection
    err = client.Ping(context.TODO(), nil)if err != nil {

    log.Fatal(err)
    }

    fmt.Println("Connected to MongoDB!")
}
```

Step 3.3: Run Your Application

Run your application using the command:

```bash
go run main.go
```

```
` ` `
```

You should see the message "Connected to MongoDB!" indicating that your Go application is successfully connected to the MongoDB server.

Step 4: CRUD Operations

In this section, we will implement the basic CRUD operations.### Step 4.1: Create
To insert a new document into a MongoDB collection, you can use the `InsertOne` method:

```go
collection := client.Database("testdb").Collection("users")

user := bson.D{
{Key: "name", Value: "John Doe"},
{Key: "age", Value: 30},
}

insertResult, err := collection.InsertOne(context.TODO(), user)if err != nil {
log.Fatal(err)
}

fmt.Printf("Inserted a single document: %v\n", insertResult.InsertedID)
` ` `
```

Step 4.2: Read

To read documents from a MongoDB collection, you can

use the `Find` method:

```go
cursor, err := collection.Find(context.TODO(),
bson.D{{}})if err != nil {
log.Fatal(err)
}
defer cursor.Close(context.TODO())

var results []bson.D
for cursor.Next(context.TODO()) {

var result bson.D
err := cursor.Decode(&result)if err != nil {
log.Fatal(err)
}
results = append(results, result)
}

fmt.Printf("Found multiple documents: %+v\n", results)
```

Step 4.3: Update

To update a document in the collection, you can use the
`UpdateOne` method:

```go
filter := bson.D{{Key: "name", Value: "John Doe"}}update
:= bson.D{
{Key: "$set", Value: bson.D{
{Key: "age", Value: 31},
}},
```

```
}

updateResult, err :=
collection.UpdateOne(context.TODO(), filter, update) if
err != nil {
log.Fatal(err)
}

fmt.Printf("Updated %v documents.\n",
updateResult.ModifiedCount)
```

Step 4.4: Delete

Finally, to delete a document, you can use the
`DeleteOne` method:

```go
deleteResult, err := collection.DeleteOne(context.TODO(),
filter)if err != nil {
log.Fatal(err)
}

fmt.Printf("Deleted %v documents.\n",
deleteResult.DeletedCount)
```

Step 5: Closing the Connection

After performing your operations, don't forget to
disconnect from the MongoDB server:

```go
```

```
err = client.Disconnect(context.TODO())if err != nil {
log.Fatal(err)
}
```

fmt.Println("Disconnected from MongoDB.")
```
``` `

Setting up MongoDB in a Go environment is straightforward and allows you to build scalable applications with ease. In this chapter, we covered the installation process, connecting to the database, and performing basic CRUD operations. With these foundational steps, you're well-equipped to incorporate MongoDB intoyour Go applications.

Querying NoSQL Databases with Go

Unlike traditional relational databases, NoSQL systems offer flexibility in schema design and are optimized for scalability, high availability, and performance. In this chapter, we'll explore how to effectively query NoSQL databases using Go, a language known for its simplicity and efficiency.

We'll cover the following NoSQL database paradigms:

Document Stores (e.g., MongoDB)
Key-Value Stores (e.g., Redis)
Wide-Column Stores (e.g., Cassandra)
Graph Databases (e.g., Neo4j)

For each type of database, we will demonstrate how to set up connections, perform basic CRUD (Create, Read,

Update, Delete) operations, and run queries.

5.1 Overview of NoSQL Databases

Before diving into querying, it is essential to recognize why NoSQL databases are becoming popular. Theirability to handle unstructured data, ease of scaling horizontally, and flexible data models make them attractive choices for modern applications.

5.1.1 Document Stores

Document stores store data in document formats, typically JSON or BSON. Each document is a self-contained unit of data. MongoDB is the most popular document store.

5.1.2 Key-Value Stores

Key-value stores use a simple key-value pair structure, where data is accessed via keys. Redis is a widely used example, known for its performance as an in-memory data structure store.

5.1.3 Wide-Column Stores

Wide-column stores store data in tables but allow for variable numbers of columns in each row. Apache Cassandra is a leading example, designed to manage large amounts of data across many servers.

5.1.4 Graph Databases

Graph databases use graph structures to represent data and its relationships, making them suitable for applications where connections are critical. Neo4j is one of the most popular graph databases.

5.2 Setting Up Your Go Environment

To interact with NoSQL databases in Go, you will need to set up several packages. Make sure you have Goinstalled on your machine. Then, create a new directory for your project and initialize a Go module:

```sh
mkdir nosql-examplecd nosql-example
go mod init nosql-example
```

ow, let's install necessary packages for the databases we'll discuss:

```sh
go get go.mongodb.org/mongo-driver/mongo go get github.com/go-redis/redis/v8
go get github.com/gocql/gocql
go get github.com/neo4j/neo4j-go-driver/v4
```

5.3 Querying Document Stores with MongoDB

MongoDB uses collections to group documents. Each document can have a different structure, allowing for flexible schema design.

5.3.1 Connecting to MongoDB

Here's how you connect to a MongoDB instance:

```go
package main

import ( "context""fmt"
"log"
"go.mongodb.org/mongo-driver/mongo"
"go.mongodb.org/mongo-driver/mongo/options"
)

func main() {
clientOptions                               :=
options.Client().ApplyURI("mongodb://localhost:27017")
client,    err    :=    mongo.Connect(context.TODO(),
clientOptions)
if err != nil { log.Fatal(err)
}

defer func() {
if err = client.Disconnect(context.TODO()); err != nil {
log.Fatal(err)
}
}()

fmt.Println("Connected to MongoDB!")
}
```

5.3.2 Performing CRUD Operations#### Create
```go
```

```go
collection := client.Database("testdb").Collection("users")
user := bson.M{"name": "Alice", "age": 30}
insertResult, err := collection.InsertOne(context.TODO(),
user)

if err != nil { log.Fatal(err)
}
fmt.Println("Inserted    a    single    document:    ",
insertResult.InsertedID)
```

Read

```go
var result bson.M
err        =        collection.FindOne(context.TODO(),
bson.M{"name": "Alice"}).Decode(&result)if err != nil {
log.Fatal(err)
}
fmt.Println("Found a single document: ", result)
```

Update

```go
updateResult,    err    :=    collection.UpdateOne(
context.TODO(),
bson.M{"name": "Alice"}, bson.M{"$set": bson.M{"age":
31}},
)
if err != nil { log.Fatal(err)
}
fmt.Printf("Matched %v documents and updated %v
```

documents.\n",   updateResult.MatchedCount,
updateResult.ModifiedCount)
```

#### Delete

```go
deleteResult, err := collection.DeleteOne(context.TODO(),
bson.M{"name": "Alice"})if err != nil {
log.Fatal(err)
}
fmt.Printf("Deleted %v documents in the collection\n",
deleteResult.DeletedCount)
```

5.4 Querying Key-Value Stores with Redis

Redis operates on a key-value paradigm and is often used
for caching and real-time analytics. ### 5.4.1 Connecting
to Redis
Here's how to connect to a Redis server:

```go
package main

import ( "context""fmt"
"log"
"github.com/go-redis/redis/v8"
)

func main() {
rdb      :=      redis.NewClient(&redis.Options{      Addr:
"localhost:6379",
```
```

```go
})
ctx := context.Background()err := rdb.Ping(ctx).Err()
if err != nil { log.Fatal(err)
}

fmt.Println("Connected to Redis!")
}
```

5.4.2 Performing Basic Operations#### Set
```go
err := rdb.Set(ctx, "key", "value", 0).Err()if err != nil {
log.Fatal(err)
}
```

Get

```go
val, err := rdb.Get(ctx, "key").Result()if err != nil {
log.Fatal(err)
}
fmt.Println("key:", val)
```

Delete

```go
err = rdb.Del(ctx, "key").Err()if err != nil {
log.Fatal(err)
}
```

5.5 Querying Wide-Column Stores with Cassandra

Cassandra allows for enormous amounts of data to be stored over multiple servers, making it resilient and scalable.

5.5.1 Connecting to Cassandra

```go
package main

import ("fmt"
"github.com/gocql/gocql"
)

func main() {
cluster := gocql.NewCluster("localhost") session, err := cluster.CreateSession()
if err != nil {panic(err)
}
defer session.Close()

fmt.Println("Connected to Cassandra!")
}
```

5.5.2 CRUD Operations#### Insert
```go
err = session.Query("INSERT INTO users (userid, name, age) VALUES (?, ?, ?)", gocql.TimeUUID(), "Bob", 25).Exec()
if err != nil { log.Fatal(err)
}
```

```
```

Select

```go
var name string
err = session.Query("SELECT name FROM users WHERE
userid = ?",userid).Consistency(gocql.One).Scan(&name)
if err != nil { log.Fatal(err)
}
fmt.Println("User's name: ", name)
```

Update and Delete

Similarly, you can perform update and delete operations using the appropriate CQL (Cassandra Query Language) queries.

5.6 Querying Graph Databases with Neo4j

Neo4j is a powerful graph database that uses a query language called Cypher.### 5.6.1 Connecting to Neo4j
```go
package main

import ("fmt"
"github.com/neo4j/neo4j-go-driver/v4/neo4j"
)

func main() {
driver, err := neo4j.NewDriver("bolt://localhost:7687",
neo4j.BasicAuth("username", "password", ""))if err != nil
```

```go
    {
        log.Fatal(err)
    }
    defer driver.Close()

    session := driver.NewSession(neo4j.SessionConfig{DatabaseName: "neo4j"})defer session.Close()

    fmt.Println("Connected to Neo4j!")
}
```

5.6.2 Performing CRUD Operations#### Create
```go
_, err = session.Run("CREATE (a:Person {name: $name})", map[string]interface{}{"name": "Charlie"}) if err != nil {
log.Fatal(err)
}
```

Read

```go
result, err := session.Run("MATCH (a:Person) WHERE a.name = $name RETURN a", map[string]interface{}{"name": "Charlie"})
if err != nil { log.Fatal(err)
}

for result.Next() {
fmt.Println("Found person: ", result.Record().Values[0])
```

```
}
```

Update and Delete

As with previous databases, you can run Cypher queries to update or delete records.

In this chapter, we reviewed how to connect and query various NoSQL databases using Go. Each database presents unique characteristics and strengths, making them suitable for different use cases. Understanding how to effectively use Go with these databases will empower you to build scalable and flexible applications.

With the foundational knowledge in querying NoSQL databases established, you are well-equipped to incorporate these systems into your projects and take advantage of their capabilities. In the next chapter, we will discuss best practices for database management and optimizing performance for large-scale applications.

Chapter 8: Testing Go Web Applications

In this chapter, we will explore various techniques and tools for testing Go web applications. This includes unit tests, integration tests, and end-to-end tests, alongside best practices to ensure your application is both reliable and efficient.

8.1 Understanding Testing Fundamentals

Before diving into specific practices and tools, it's important to understand the fundamental types of tests and their purposes:

Unit Tests: These tests focus on individual components of your application. They check the correctness of functions and methods to ensure they behave as expected in isolation. Unit tests in Go are typically written in the same file as the code but within a separate `_test.go` file.

Integration Tests: These tests validate the interaction between multiple components or services within your application. Integration tests are particularly important in web applications, as they ensure that different parts of your application work correctly together.

End-to-End Tests: These tests simulate user interactions with the application, testing the entire stack—from the front end through to the database. They are essential for validating the user experience and are often performed using browser automation tools.

8.2 Unit Testing in Go

Go's built-in testing framework simplifies the process of writing and running unit tests. Here's a simple example of how to write a unit test for a basic HTTP handler function:

```go
package main

import ( "net/http"
"net/http/httptest""testing"
)

func    HelloHandler(w    http.ResponseWriter,    r
*http.Request) {w.Write([]byte("Hello, world!"))
}

func TestHelloHandler(t *testing.T) {
req, err := http.NewRequest("GET", "/hello", nil)if err !=
nil {
t.Fatal(err)
}

// Create a ResponseRecorder to record the responserr :=
httptest.NewRecorder()
handler := http.HandlerFunc(HelloHandler)
```

```
// Call the handler with the request and the recorder
handler.ServeHTTP(rr, req)

// Check the status code
if status := rr.Code; status != http.StatusOK {
t.Errorf("expected status code 200, got %v", status)
}

// Check the response body expected := "Hello, world!"
if rr.Body.String() != expected {
t.Errorf("expected response body %q, got %q", expected,
rr.Body.String())
}
}
```

8.2.1 Running Unit Tests

You can run your tests using the `go test` command. By default, `go test` will look for all `_test.go` files in your package and execute the tests defined in them:

```bash
go test -v
```

The `-v` flag stands for verbose mode, which provides detailed output about the tests that were run. ## 8.3 Integration Testing

Integration tests often require a different setup, especially if your application interacts with databases or external APIs. In Go, you may want to use tools such as Docker to spin up a database instance specifically for tests.

8.3.1 Example of Integration Testing

Consider a web application that stores user information in a database. Below is an example of how to test a function that interacts with the database:

```go
package main

import ( "database/sql""log" "net/http"
"net/http/httptest""testing"

_ "github.com/lib/pq"
)

func TestCreateUser(t *testing.T) {
// Setup database connection
db, err := sql.Open("postgres", "dbname=testdb sslmode=disable")

if err != nil { log.Fatal(err)
}
defer db.Close()

// Reset the database before the test
_, err = db.Exec("DELETE FROM users")if err != nil {
t.Fatal(err)
}

req, err := http.NewRequest("POST", "/users", nil) // Assume we have a valid user payloadif err != nil {
t.Fatal(err)
}
```

```
rr := httptest.NewRecorder()
handler    :=    http.HandlerFunc(CreateUserHandler)
handler.ServeHTTP(rr, req)
if status := rr.Code; status != http.StatusCreated {
t.Errorf("expected status code 201, got %v", status)
}

// Validate the user was created in the databasevar count
int
err    =    db.QueryRow("SELECT    COUNT(*)    FROM
users").Scan(&count)if err != nil {
t.Fatal(err)
}
if count != 1 {
t.Errorf("expected 1 user in the database, got %d", count)
}
}
```
```

## 8.4 End-to-End Testing

End-to-end testing is crucial for validating that the
application flows correctly from the user's perspective. In
Go, you can leverage tools like **Selenium** or
**Playwright** for browser automation, or you could use
**Cypress** for a JavaScript-based solution. ### 8.4.1
Using Go for E2E Testing
While Go does not directly provide features for web UI
testing, you can combine Go with other tools. Below is an
example of how you might integrate your Go application
with a headless browser using `chromedp`:
```

```go
package main

import ( "context""fmt"

"github.com/chromedp/chromedp""testing"
)

func TestHomepage(t *testing.T) {
ctx,                        cancel                        :=
chromedp.NewContext(context.Background())      defer
cancel()

var title string
err                    :=                    chromedp.Run(ctx,
chromedp.Navigate("http://localhost:8080"),
chromedp.Title(&title),
)
if err != nil {t.Fatal(err)
}

if title != "Expected Page Title" {
t.Errorf("expected title to be 'Expected Page Title', got
'%s'", title)
}
}
```

8.5 Best Practices for Testing Go Web Applications

Test Coverage: Utilize Go's testing tool to measure coverage. You can run tests with `go test -cover` to see how much of your codebase is covered by tests.

Mock External Services: When your application relies on external services (e.g., APIs, third-party libraries), consider using mocks or stubs to isolate tests.

CI/CD Integration: Integrate your tests into a Continuous Integration/Continuous Deploymentpipeline to ensure automated testing on every code push.

Keep Tests Independent: Tests should not depend on each other or rely on external states. Each testshould run independently to ensure reliability.

Clear Test Targets: Structure your tests clearly. Utilize table-driven tests for testing multiple scenarios within a single test function.

Use Descriptive Names: Name your tests descriptively so that their purpose is clear. Follow namingconventions such as `TestFunctionName_Scenario`.

Testing Go web applications doesn't have to be daunting. With Go's powerful testing capabilities and a clear understanding of your testing strategy, you can ensure that your applications meet quality standards. In this chapter, we explored the fundamentals of unit, integration, and end-to-end testing, provided practical examples, and discussed best practices. By adopting these techniques, you will be well-equipped to deliver reliable and maintainable Go web applications.

Writing Unit Tests for Go Code

In the Go programming language (often referred to as Golang), writing unit tests is straightforward and well-integrated into the development workflow. This chapter will introduce you to the fundamentals of writing unit tests for Go code, exploring testing frameworks, strategies, and best practices that can help you produce robust and reliable applications.

Why Write Unit Tests?

Unit tests serve several key purposes:

Catch Bugs Early: By testing individual components of your code in isolation, you can identify and fix bugs before they propagate to later stages of development.

Document Code Behavior: Tests act as a living documentation. They illustrate how functions are expected to behave under various conditions.

Refactor with Confidence: If you have a comprehensive suite of unit tests, you can refactor code with the reassurance that existing functionality will remain intact.

Improve Design: Writing tests can lead to cleaner, more modular code as you are forced to think about dependencies and interactions between components.

Facilitate Collaboration: With a solid test suite in

place, teams can work together more efficiently, knowing that changes can be validated quickly.

Setting Up Your Go Testing Environment

Go has a built-in testing framework that simplifies the process of writing and running tests. To get started, ensure you have Go installed on your machine and set up your Go workspace properly. The basic structure of a Go project typically follows:

```
/my-go-projectmain.go main_test.go
...
```

In this setup, `main.go` contains your application code, while `main_test.go` is where your tests for the code in `main.go` will reside.

Writing Your First Unit Test

Here's a simple example to illustrate how to write a unit test in Go. Suppose we have a function that adds two integers:

```go
// main.go package main

import "fmt"

func Add(a, b int) int {return a + b
}
```

```go
func main() { fmt.Println(Add(2, 3))
}
```

The corresponding test file would look like this:

```go
// main_test.gopackage main

import "testing"

func TestAdd(t *testing.T) {result := Add(2, 3) expected :=
5

if result != expected {
t.Errorf("Add(2, 3) = %d; expected %d", result, expected)
}
}
```

Understanding the Test

The test function `TestAdd` is named based on the convention that the name should start with `Test` followed by the function name being tested.
The `testing.T` parameter provides methods to log and signal test failures.
The `t.Errorf` method is used to report a failure when the actual outcome does not match the expectedoutcome.

Running Your Tests

To execute your tests, use the `go test` command in your terminal:

```bash
go test
```

This command automatically searches for any files ending in `_test.go` within the current package, compiles the test files, and runs the tests. You should see output indicating whether your tests passed or failed.

Testing Different Scenarios

It is vital to test multiple scenarios to ensure your functions behave as expected under various conditions. Here's an example of testing different inputs:

```go
// main_test.go

package main import "testing"
func TestAdd(t *testing.T) {tests := []struct {
a, b    int expected int
}{
{1, 2, 3},
{2, 3, 5},
{10, 5, 15},
{-1, -1, -2},
{0, 0, 0},
}

for _, test := range tests { result := Add(test.a, test.b) if
result != test.expected {
```

```
        t.Errorf("Add(%d, %d) = %d; expected %d", test.a, test.b,
        result, test.expected)
        }
    }
}
```

In this example, we define a struct to hold our test cases,
allowing us to iterate over different input pairs and
expected results.

Test Coverage

Testing is not just about writing tests; it's also important
to ensure you are testing enough of your codebase. Go
provides a tool to measure test coverage. You can run:

```bash
go test -cover
```

This command will return a report indicating the
percentage of code covered by your tests. Aim for high
coverage but remember that 100% coverage does not
equal zero bugs.

Best Practices for Writing Unit Tests

Keep Tests Isolated: Each test should be independent
of others to ensure reliability andreproducibility.

Use Descriptive Names: Test function names should
clearly indicate what the test is verifying.

Avoid Side Effects: Tests should not modify shared variables or state to prevent interference between tests.

Test Edge Cases: Cover edge cases and potential failure modes to ensure your code can handle unexpected inputs.

Run Tests Frequently: Incorporate testing into your regular development workflow to catch issues early.

Mock Dependencies: For functions that rely on external systems (like databases or APIs), use mocking to isolate your tests and avoid side effects.

By following the principles outlined in this chapter, new and experienced Go developers alike can build a strong foundation in testing. Embrace unit testing as an integral part of your development process, and enjoy the increased confidence and clarity it brings to your coding journey. As you become more familiar with writing tests, you will find that they not only catch bugs but also enhance your overall approach to software design.

Integrating Go Testing Frameworks

In the Go programming language, testing is a first-class citizen. The standard library provides a comprehensive testing package, making it easier to write and run tests. However, as applications grow in complexity, developers often find the need to integrate additional testing frameworks to augment the built-in capabilities. In this chapter, we'll explore how to integrate various Go testing frameworks, enhance testing coverage, and streamline the testing workflow.

The Go Testing Package

Before diving into integration, it's important to familiarize ourselves with Go's built-in testing capabilities. The standard `testing` package provides the foundation for writing unit tests in Go. Here's a brief overview of its components:

Test Functions: Functions that start with `Test` followed by a name (e.g., `TestAdd`) are executed by the testing framework.
Benchmark Functions: Functions that start with `Benchmark` (e.g., `BenchmarkAdd`) are used to measure performance.
Example Functions: Functions starting with `Example` are used to provide example output for documentation.

A simple Go test might look as follows:

```go
package math import "testing"
func Add(a, b int) int {return a + b
}

func TestAdd(t *testing.T) {result := Add(2, 3) expected :=
5

if result != expected {
t.Errorf("Expected %d, but got %d", expected, result)
```

```
    }
  }
```

To run the tests, you'll typically use `go test` in the terminal, which will automatically discover and run the test functions defined in your package.

Popular Go Testing Frameworks

While the built-in `testing` package is sufficient for many use cases, there are several third-party frameworks that can enhance the testing experience in Go:

Testify: Provides assertions, mock objects, and a suite of testing tools that simplify writing and maintaining tests.
Ginkgo: A BDD (Behavior-Driven Development) framework that allows for more structured and descriptive test definitions.
GoMock: An excellent tool for mocking interfaces, which is particularly useful in unit testing. ## Integrating Testify
To integrate Testify, first, install it using `go get`:

```bash
go get github.com/stretchr/testify
```

Next, you can leverage its powerful assertion methods to write cleaner tests. Here's how you can modify the previous example using Testify's assertions:

```go
```

```go
package math

import ( "testing"
"github.com/stretchr/testify/assert"
)

func TestAdd(t *testing.T) {result := Add(2, 3)
assert.Equal(t, 5, result, "they should be equal")
}
```

This allows you to write more readable tests while reducing boilerplate code.## Integrating Ginkgo
To use Ginkgo, first install it along with Gomega (its matcher library):

```bash
go get github.com/onsi/ginkgo/ginkgo go get github.com/onsi/gomega
```

Creating a Ginkgo test requires a slightly different structure:

```go
package math_test

import ( "math"
. "github.com/onsi/ginkgo"
. "github.com/onsi/gomega"
)

var _ = Describe("Math", func() { Context("Addition",
```

```
func() { It("adds 2 and 3", func() {
result := math.Add(2, 3) Expect(result).To(Equal(5))
})
})
})
```

Ginkgo provides a rich set of features, including hierarchical organization of tests and the ability to define setup and teardown procedures for individual tests or suites.

Integrating GoMock

To use GoMock, install it via:

```bash
go get github.com/golang/mock/gomock
```

You also need to install `mockgen`, which generates mock interfaces:

```bash
go install github.com/golang/mock/mockgen@latest
```

With GoMock, you first generate a mock of your target interface. Suppose you have an interface `Calculator`:

```go
package calculator
```

```go
type Calculator interface {Add(a, b int) int
}
```

You would generate a mock using `mockgen`, and then use that mock in your tests:

```go
package calculator_test

import ( "testing"
"github.com/golang/mock/gomock"
"github.com/yourusername/project/calculator"
"github.com/yourusername/project/calculator/mocks"
)

func TestAdd(t *testing.T) {
ctrl := gomock.NewController(t)defer ctrl.Finish()

mockCalc       :=        mocks.NewMockCalculator(ctrl)
mockCalc.EXPECT().Add(2, 3).Return(5)

result := mockCalc.Add(2, 3)if result != 5 {
t.Errorf("Expected 5, but got %d", result)
}
}
```

Best Practices for Integration

Choose the Right Frameworks: Depending on your project needs, select the frameworks that best match your

testing philosophy (e.g., BDD vs. traditional testing).
Keep Tests Isolated: Ensure that tests are independent of each other, making it easier to identify failures.
Use Mocks Wisely: While mocking is powerful, avoid overusing it to ensure you're testing the actual interactions in your code.
Stay Consistent: Use a consistent structure across your tests to improve readability and maintainability.

Integrating additional testing frameworks into your Go project can significantly enhance your ability to write tests that are more expressive, easier to maintain, and capable of thorough coverage. Whether you choose Testify for its assertions, Ginkgo for its BDD capabilities, or GoMock for interface mocking, each framework brings unique strengths to the table. By carefully selecting the right tools and following best practices, you can create a robust testing environment that fosters high-quality software development.

Chapter 9: Securing Your Web Server Applications

With the rise in cyberattacks and data breaches, developers and organizations must prioritize security to protect their users and data. In this chapter, we will explore various best practices, strategies, and tools for securing your web server applications written in Go (Golang). We'll cover fundamental security concepts, how to secure APIs, manage authentication and authorization, and much more.

9.1 Understanding the Security Landscape

Before diving into specific security measures, it's essential to understand the potential threats your web applications face. Common vulnerabilities in web applications include:

SQL Injection: Attackers can manipulate queries to access unauthorized data.
Cross-Site Scripting (XSS): Malicious scripts can be executed in the context of the user's browser.
Cross-Site Request Forgery (CSRF): This attack tricks users into performing actions they did not intend.
Insecure Direct Object References (IDOR): Attackers can gain access to objects by modifying URL parameters.
Denial of Service (DoS): Overloading your server with requests can render your service unavailable. By knowing these vulnerabilities, you can better prepare your applications to withstand attacks.
9.2 Best Practices for Securing Go Web Applications
9.2.1 Input Validation and Sanitization

Always validate and sanitize user input, as malicious users can insert harmful data. Use Go's built-in packages and libraries to validate data effectively. Here is a simple example of validating an email address:

```go
import (
"net/mail""log"
)

func validateEmail(email string) bool {
_, err := mail.ParseAddress(email)return err == nil
}

// Usage
email := "test@example.com"if !validateEmail(email) {
log.Println("Invalid email address")
}
```

9.2.2 Output Encoding

To protect against XSS attacks, ensure to encode output that will be displayed in the browser. Libraries like `html/template` in Go can automatically escape potentially dangerous content.

```go
import (
"html/template""net/http"
)

func handler(w http.ResponseWriter, r *http.Request) {
name := r.URL.Query().Get("name")
tmpl                                                     :=
```

```
template.Must(template.New("hello").Parse("<h1>Hello,
{{.}}!</h1>"))tmpl.Execute(w, name) // The name will be
automatically escaped.
}
```

9.2.3 Authentication and Authorization

Implementing a robust authentication mechanism is
crucial. Use proven libraries like
`golang.org/x/crypto/bcrypt` for password hashing:

```go
import (
"golang.org/x/crypto/bcrypt"
)

func hashPassword(password string) (string, error) {
hashedBytes, err :=
bcrypt.GenerateFromPassword([]byte(password),
bcrypt.DefaultCost)return string(hashedBytes), err
}

func checkPasswordHash(password, hash string) bool {
return bcrypt.CompareHashAndPassword([]byte(hash),
[]byte(password)) == nil
}
```

For web applications, consider using JWT (JSON Web
Tokens) to manage sessions and authorize users
efficiently.

9.2.4 Rate Limiting

To defend against DoS attacks and brute-force login attempts, implement rate limiting. You can use middleware to track requests from users and apply thresholds.

```go
go import (
"net/http""time"
)

var requestCount = make(map[string]int)
var lastRequestTime = make(map[string]time.Time)

func     rateLimitMiddleware(next     http.Handler)
http.Handler {
return http.HandlerFunc(func(w http.ResponseWriter, r
*http.Request) {ip := r.RemoteAddr
currentTime := time.Now()

if             lastRequestTime[ip].Add(1          *
time.Minute).Before(currentTime) {requestCount[ip] = 0
lastRequestTime[ip] = currentTime
}

requestCount[ip]++
if requestCount[ip] > 100 { // Limit to 100 requests per
minute    http.Error(w,    "Too    Many    Requests",
http.StatusTooManyRequests)return
}

next.ServeHTTP(w, r)
})
}
```

```
```

9.2.5 Secure Communication

Always use HTTPS to secure data in transit. Obtain an SSL/TLS certificate and ensure that your server is configured to redirect HTTP to HTTPS.

9.2.6 Error Handling

Avoid revealing sensitive information through error messages. Generic error messages should be shown to users, while detailed errors can be logged for development purposes.

```go
func myHandler(w http.ResponseWriter, r *http.Request) {
// Processing...

if err != nil {
log.Printf("Error processing request: %v", err)
http.Error(w, "Internal Server Error", http.StatusInternalServerError)return
}
}
```

9.2.7 Regular Security Audits

Finally, perform regular security audits on your application. Tools like `gosec` can analyze your code for known vulnerabilities.

```bash
go get github.com/securego/gosec/v2gosec ./...
```

Securing your web application is an ongoing process that requires a deep understanding of potential vulnerabilities and effective implementation of security practices. As developers, it's our responsibility to prioritize security at all stages of application development, from design to deployment. By adhering to the best practices outlined in this chapter, you can significantly reduce the risk of threats and build robust, secureweb server applications in Go.

Authentication and Authorization Strategies in Go

Thus, implementing robust authentication and authorization strategies is essential. This chapter focuses on how to effectively implement these strategies in Go (Golang), a language known for its performance, simplicity, and efficiency.

Understanding Authentication and Authorization

Before diving into the implementation, it is crucial to differentiate between authentication and authorization:

Authentication is the process of verifying the identity of a user or system. It answers the question: "Who are you?"
Authorization checks what an authenticated user is

allowed to do. It answers the question: "What can you do?"

A secure application must utilize both strategies, ensuring that only legitimate users are granted access to functionalities suited to their roles.

Common Authentication Strategies ### 1. Basic Authentication
Basic Authentication is one of the simplest forms of authentication, involving sending a username and password encoded in Base64. To implement this in Go, you can utilize the `http` package:

```go
package main

import (
"encoding/base64""net/http" "strings"
)

func basicAuth(next http.Handler) http.Handler {
return http.HandlerFunc(func(w http.ResponseWriter, r *http.Request)          {          authHeader          :=
r.Header.Get("Authorization")
if authHeader == "" {
w.Header().Set("WWW-Authenticate",          "Basic")
http.Error(w, "Unauthorized", http.StatusUnauthorized)
return
}

// Parse the credentials
payload   :=   strings.SplitN(authHeader,   "   ",   2) if
len(payload) != 2 || payload[0] != "Basic" {
```

```go
			http.Error(w, "Unauthorized", http.StatusUnauthorized)
			return
		}
		credentials, err := base64.StdEncoding.DecodeString(payload[1])
		if err != nil {

			http.Error(w, "Unauthorized", http.StatusUnauthorized)
			return
		}

		parts := strings.SplitN(string(credentials), ":", 2)
		if len(parts) != 2 || !validateCredentials(parts[0], parts[1]) {
			http.Error(w, "Unauthorized", http.StatusUnauthorized)
			return
		}

		next.ServeHTTP(w, r)
	})
}

func validateCredentials(username, password string) bool {
	// Replace with actual validation
	return username == "user" && password == "password"
}
```

2. Token-Based Authentication

Token-based authentication is more secure than Basic Authentication and is commonly used in RESTful APIs. The most common implementation uses JSON Web

Tokens (JWTs).

To use JWT in Go, the `github.com/dgrijalva/jwt-go` library is popular:

```go
package main

import (
"fmt" "github.com/dgrijalva/jwt-go""net/http"
"time"
)
var hmacSampleSecret = []byte("my_secret_key") func generateJWT(username string) (string, error) {
expirationTime := time.Now().Add(5 * time.Minute)
claims := &jwt.StandardClaims{
ExpiresAt: expirationTime.Unix(),Issuer:     username,
}

token := jwt.NewWithClaims(jwt.SigningMethodHS256, claims)return token.SignedString(hmacSampleSecret)
}

func jwtAuth(next http.Handler) http.Handler {
return http.HandlerFunc(func(w http.ResponseWriter, r *http.Request)       {       authToken       := r.Header.Get("Authorization")
if authToken == "" {
```

```go
			http.Error(w, "Unauthorized", http.StatusUnauthorized)
			return
		}

		token, err := jwt.Parse(authToken, func(token *jwt.Token) (interface{}, error) { return hmacSampleSecret, nil
		})

		if err != nil || !token.Valid {
			http.Error(w, "Unauthorized", http.StatusUnauthorized)
			return



		})
		}
```

		}

		next.ServeHTTP(w, r)

3. OAuth2

OAuth2 is a widely-used authorization framework that allows third-party applications to obtain limited access to a user's resources without exposing credentials. In Go, `golang.org/x/oauth2` provides a library for handling OAuth2 flows.

```go
```

```go
package main

import (
"golang.org/x/oauth2"     "golang.org/x/oauth2/google"
"net/http"
)

var (
oauth2Config     =     &oauth2.Config{     ClientID:
    "YOUR_CLIENT_ID",
ClientSecret: "YOUR_CLIENT_SECRET", RedirectURL:
"http://localhost:8080/callback",
Scopes:
    []string{"https://www.googleapis.com/auth/userin
fo.profile"}, Endpoint:        google.Endpoint,
}
)

func   handleGoogleLogin(w   http.ResponseWriter,   r
*http.Request) {
url     :=     oauth2Config.AuthCodeURL("state",
oauth2.AccessTypeOffline)   http.Redirect(w,   r,   url,
http.StatusTemporaryRedirect)
}

func   handleGoogleCallback(w   http.ResponseWriter,   r
*http.Request) {code := r.URL.Query().Get("code")
// Exchange code for a token...
}
```
```

## Authorization Strategies
```

Once you have users authenticated, the next step is managing their access to different functionalities within your application.

Role-Based Access Control (RBAC)

RBAC is a common strategy where permissions are assigned to roles, and roles are assigned to users. This separation allows for easier management of user permissions.

Here's a simple implementation of RBAC in Go:

```go
type Role string

const (
Admin Role = "admin"User Role = "user"
)

type User struct { Username stringRole  Role
}

var userDB = map[string]User{"user1": {"user1", Admin},
"user2": {"user2", User},
}

func authorize(role Role) http.Handler {
return http.HandlerFunc(func(w http.ResponseWriter, r *http.Request)            {            username            := r.Context().Value("username").(string)
user, exists := userDB[username]
```

```
if !exists || user.Role != role {
http.Error(w, "Forbidden", http.StatusForbidden)return
}
})
}
```

Attribute-Based Access Control (ABAC)

ABAC is a more fine-grained approach compared to RBAC, as it considers various attributes (user attributes, resource attributes, etc.) for access control decisions. In Go, you can create middleware that evaluates user attributes against resource attributes.

Best Practices

Use HTTPS: Always ensure that all communications are conducted over HTTPS to preventeavesdropping.
Secure storage of credentials: Passwords should always be hashed and not stored in plain text.

Implement rate limiting: To prevent brute-force attacks, you should add mechanisms to limit thenumber of authentication attempts.
Regularly review and update access controls: Ensure that users have only the access they require andremove inactive accounts promptly.
Utilize frameworks or libraries: Where possible, leverage existing libraries as they reduce thecomplexity of implementation and increase security through community review.

Authentication and authorization are critical components of any secure application. Go offers a range of strategies and libraries to implement these mechanisms effectively. Understanding these options and their applications will not only ensure that your applications are secure but also enhance the user experience as they interact with your services. The next steps involve deciding on the most appropriate strategies for your particular use case and implementing them diligently.

Handling HTTPS and Secure Connections

Data breaches, man-in-the-middle attacks, and eavesdropping are real threats that can compromise sensitiveinformation. Therefore, having a grasp of secure connections, particularly through HTTPS, is essential for developers working with Go.

Understanding HTTPS

HyperText Transfer Protocol Secure (HTTPS) is the secure version of HTTP, utilizing Transport Layer Security (TLS) to encrypt the data transmitted between the client and the server. This encryption ensures that sensitive information such as login credentials, financial data, and personal information cannot be intercepted by malicious actors.

The Role of TLS

Transport Layer Security (TLS) provides three main security properties:

Confidentiality: Data is encrypted, making it unreadable if intercepted.
Integrity: Ensures that data hasn't been tampered with during transit.
Authentication: Verifies the identity of the communicating parties.

With HTTPS, a secure channel is established between the user's web browser (client) and the server, using TLS to encrypt the data exchanged.

Setting Up HTTPS in Go

Setting up HTTPS in a Go application is straightforward, thanks to the `net/http` and `crypto/tls` packages provided in the standard library.

Creating a Self-Signed Certificate for Testing

For local development, you may use a self-signed certificate. However, for production, always obtain a certificate signed by a trusted certificate authority (CA).

Below are the steps to create a self-signed certificate:

Create a private key:
```bash
openssl genrsa -out server.key 2048
```

Create a certificate signing request (CSR):
```bash
openssl req -new -key server.key -out server.csr
```

```
```

Generate the self-signed certificate:
```bash
openssl x509 -req -days 365 -in server.csr -signkey server.key -out server.crt
```

Writing a Simple HTTPS Server

Let's create a simple HTTPS server using the generated certificate.

```go
package main

import ( "fmt" "net/http"
)

func handler(w http.ResponseWriter, r *http.Request) {
fmt.Fprintf(w, "Hello, HTTPS!")
}

func main() { http.HandleFunc("/", handler)

// Start the server on port 443
err := http.ListenAndServeTLS(":443", "server.crt", "server.key", nil)if err != nil {
panic(err)
}
}
```

Starting the Server

To run the server, execute the following command:
```bash
sudo go run main.go
```

Make sure to run it with root privileges (using `sudo` on Unix-like systems) since ports below 1024 require elevated permissions.

You can now access your server at `https://localhost`, where your browser may warn you that it is insecure due to a self-signed certificate. In a production scenario, you would use a valid certificate obtained from a trusted CA.

Handling HTTPS Clients

The Go standard library also makes it simple to make HTTPS requests using the `http` package. Here's how to perform a secure GET request to an HTTPS endpoint.

Making HTTPS Requests

```go
package main

import ( "crypto/tls""fmt" "net/http"
)

func main() {
// Create a new HTTP client with default settingsclient :=
&http.Client{
```

```
Transport:          &http.Transport{          TLSClientConfig:
&tls.Config{
InsecureSkipVerify: true, // Not recommended for
production
},
},
}

resp, err := client.Get("https://localhost")if err != nil {
panic(err)
}
defer resp.Body.Close()

fmt.Println("Response Status:", resp.Status)
}
```

TLS Configuration Options

When creating a custom `tls.Config`, you can specify various parameters to fine-tune the security features of your connections:
MinVersion: To enforce a minimum TLS version.
RootCAs: A set of trusted root certificate authorities.
Certificates: For providing client-side certificates if mutual authentication is required.## Best Practices for HTTPS in Go
Use Strong Security Settings

When configuring TLS settings, ensure strong security settings by:
Enforcing the latest TLS versions.
Implementing `Strict-Transport-Security` HTTP headers.

Regularly updating your Go dependencies, particularly cryptographic libraries. ### Avoid InsecureSkipVerify in Production
The `InsecureSkipVerify` option in TLS configuration disables verification of the server's certificate chain and host name, exposing the client to potential risks. Always ensure proper verification in production environments.

Monitoring and Testing

Regularly monitor your application for vulnerabilities. Utilize tools like [SSL Labs](https://www.ssllabs.com/ssltest/) to test your server's TLS configuration and make necessary adjustments.

By understanding the principles of HTTPS and using the tools provided effectively, developers can create secure applications that protect users' data and maintain the integrity of communications. As developers, it is our responsibility to prioritize security by implementing best practices and staying updated with the latest security measures. Embrace HTTPS, and ensure your Go applications are secure in today's digital landscape.

Chapter 10: Deploying Web Applications with Cutting-Edge Tools

The landscape of web application deployment has undergone significant transformation, driven by advancements in technology, best practices, and the demand for rapid, reliable, and scalable solutions. This chapter will explore modern deployment methodologies, tools, and strategies that facilitate the seamless launch of web applications in today's fast-paced environment.

1. Understanding Deployment: A Critical Step in Development

Deployment refers to the process of making a web application available for users. While it may appear straightforward, several factors influence successful deployment, including:

Infrastructure Management: Choosing the right cloud services or servers.
Version Control: Ensuring that the correct version of the application is deployed.
Automated Testing: Verifying that the application behaves as expected before going live.
Scalability: Preparing the application to handle varying loads.
Security: Safeguarding user data and maintaining compliance with regulations. ## 2. Modern Deployment Strategies
2.1 Continuous Integration/Continuous Deployment (CI/CD)

The CI/CD approach has revolutionized how organizations deploy applications. Continuous Integration involves frequently merging code changes into a shared repository, where automated builds and tests are triggered. Continuous Deployment takes it a step further by automatically deploying code changes to production after passing tests.

Tools to Use:
Jenkins: An open-source automation server that facilitates CI/CD pipelines.
GitLab CI/CD: Integrated tools that work seamlessly with version control.

2.2 Containerization
Containerization allows developers to package applications and their dependencies into containers, ensuring consistency across different environments. This makes it easier to deploy applications anywhere, from developer laptops to cloud servers.

Tools to Use:
Docker: The most popular containerization platform, enabling quick deployment and scalability.
Kubernetes: An orchestration tool for managing containerized applications, ideal for production environments.

2.3 Infrastructure as Code (IaC)

Infrastructure as Code allows developers to manage and provision resources through code. It streamlines the setup of infrastructure while promoting standardization and reducing the risk of human error.

Tools to Use:
Terraform: A powerful tool that enables users to define and provision infrastructure using declarative configuration files.

AWS CloudFormation: A service that helps create and manage AWS resources using templates.

3. Deploying on Cloud Platforms
The advent of cloud computing has transformed deployment capabilities,
offering scalability and flexibility. Leading cloud service providers offer multiple specialized services tailored for web applications.

3.1 Amazon Web Services (AWS)

AWS provides a comprehensive suite of tools for deploying web applications, including:
Elastic Beanstalk: A platform-as-a-service (PaaS) that automates deployment, from capacity provisioning to application health monitoring.
Lambda: Enables serverless computing, allowing developers to run code without provisioning or managing servers.

3.2 Microsoft Azure

Azure offers robust services for web application deployment, such as:
Azure App Service: A fully managed platform for building, deploying, and scaling web apps.
Azure Functions: A serverless compute service that

helps developers run event-driven code. ### 3.3 Google Cloud Platform (GCP)

GCP is another key player, featuring:

App Engine: A platform for building and hosting applications in Google-managed data centers.

Cloud Run: A fully managed compute platform that allows you to run containers in a serverless environment.

4. Best Practices for Modern Deployment ### 4.1 Automated Testing

Implement a robust suite of automated tests to identify issues before going live. This includes unit tests, integration tests, and end-to-end tests.

4.2 Monitoring and Logging

Once your application is deployed, continuous monitoring is vital. Utilize tools like Prometheus and Grafana for real-time monitoring and logging frameworks like ELK Stack (Elasticsearch, Logstash, and Kibana) to analyze application performance.

4.3 Rollback Strategies

Always prepare strategies for rollback in case of deployment failures. Blue/Green deployments and Canary releases are effective methodologies that allow you to minimize risks.

4.4 Security Measures

Incorporate security measures, such as API gateways, SSL certificates, and regular vulnerability assessments, as part of the deployment process.

5. Future Trends in Web Application Deployment

The landscape of web application deployment is continuously evolving. Emerging trends include:

Serverless Architectures: Emphasizing event-driven models that minimize server management.
Multi-Cloud Strategies: Businesses are increasingly adopting multi-cloud environments to prevent vendor lock-in and enhance resilience.
Machine Learning Operations (MLOps): Leveraging AI and ML in the deployment process for better performance prediction and resource management.

Deploying web applications is a complex yet crucial aspect of development that demands an understanding of modern tools, strategies, and best practices. By embracing cutting-edge technologies and methodologies, developers and organizations can ensure that their applications are not only deployed efficiently but also maintained and scaled effectively in the long run. As the field continues to evolve, staying abreast of innovative deployment strategies will be essential for success in the digital landscape.

Building Docker Containers for Go Applications

In this chapter, we will explore how to build Docker containers for Go applications, from the initial setup to deploying and running these containers effectively.

Why Use Docker for Go Applications?

Go, also known as Golang, is a statically typed, compiled programming language designed for simplicity and efficiency. Its lightweight nature makes it an excellent candidate for containerization. However, there are several reasons to use Docker for Go applications:

Consistency across Environments: Docker containers ensure that your application runs in the sameenvironment across development, testing, and production.

Simplified Dependencies: Go programs often depend on various libraries and tools. Docker enables you to encapsulate these dependencies within the container, eliminating conflicts.

Portability: With Docker, you can easily move your applications between different systems, cloudproviders, or environments without worrying about the underlying infrastructure.

Scalability: Docker integrates well with orchestration tools like Kubernetes, facilitating the scaling of Go applications as demand grows.

Prerequisites

Before diving into building Docker containers for Go applications, ensure you have the followingprerequisites:

Go Installed: Make sure you have Go installed on your machine. You can download it from theofficial Go website at [golang.org](https://golang.org/dl/).

Docker Installed: Install Docker by following the instructions on the official Docker website at [docker.com](https://docs.docker.com/get-docker/).

Basic Knowledge of Go: Familiarity with Go programming concepts is essential to build and manage your applications.

Creating a Simple Go Application

Let's start by creating a simple Go application. Open your terminal or command prompt and execute the following steps.

Set Up the Project Directory:
```bash
mkdir hello-gocd hello-go
```

Create the Main Go File:
Create a file named `main.go` with the following content. This simple application returns "Hello, World!" when accessed.

```go
package main

import (
"fmt" "net/http"
)

func    helloWorldHandler(w    http.ResponseWriter,    r
```

```
*http.Request) {fmt.Fprintf(w, "Hello, World!")
}

func main() {
http.HandleFunc("/",              helloWorldHandler)
http.ListenAndServe(":8080", nil)
}
```

Testing the Application Locally:
You can run your application locally to ensure it's working.
```bash
go run main.go
```

Open a browser and navigate to `http://localhost:8080`, where you should see "Hello, World!" ## Writing a Dockerfile
The next step is to write a Dockerfile. A Dockerfile is a script containing instructions for building a Docker image. Create a file named `Dockerfile` in your project directory and add the following content:

```Dockerfile
# Use the official Go image as the base image FROM golang:1.20 AS builder

# Set the working directory inside the container
WORKDIR /app

# Copy the Go modules and download the dependencies
COPY go.mod go.sum ./
RUN go mod download
```

Copy the source code into the containerCOPY . .

Build the Go application
RUN CGO_ENABLED=0 GOOS=linux go build -o app .

Start a new stage from a smaller image FROM alpine:latest

Set the working directoryWORKDIR /root/

Copy the binary from the builder stage COPY --from=builder /app/app .

Expose the port on which the app will run EXPOSE 8080

Command to run the executableCMD ["./app"]
```

### Breakdown of the Dockerfile

**Base Image**: We start with the official Go image for building the application.
**Working Directory**: We set the working directory to `/app` inside the container.
**Dependency Management**: We copy over the `go.mod` and `go.sum` files before the actual source code to leverage Docker's caching mechanism, ensuring faster builds when code changes but dependenciesdo not.
**Building the Application**: We build the Go application using the `go build` command. The `CGO_ENABLED=0` and `GOOS=linux` flags ensure the
```

binary is statically linked and portable.
Final Image: We switch to a smaller base image (`alpine`) for the production container, which keeps the final image lightweight.
Exposing the Port: We expose port 8080 to make the application accessible.
Command to Run: Finally, we provide the command to run the compiled application. ## Building the Docker Image
With the Dockerfile ready, you can now build your Docker image. Run the following command in your terminal from the project directory:

```bash
docker build -t hello-go .
```

This command tells Docker to build an image named `hello-go` using the current directory (`.`) as the build context. Depending on your setup and the size of your Go application, this command could take a few moments to complete.

Running the Docker Container

After successfully building the image, you can now run your Go application inside a Docker container:

```bash
docker run -p 8080:8080 hello-go
```

This command will:

Start a new container from the `hello-go` image.
Map port `8080` of the container to port `8080` of your localhost, allowing you to access the application in your web browser.

Visit `http://localhost:8080` in your browser, and you should see the "Hello, World!" message again, now served from within a Docker container!

In this chapter, we explored how to build Docker containers for Go applications. We started with a simple Go web application, created a Dockerfile to containerize it, and then built and ran our Docker container. Docker not only simplifies the deployment process but also enhances the portability and scalability of Go applications.

Configuring CI/CD Pipelines for Go

Continuous Integration (CI) and Continuous Deployment (CD) are essential practices in modern software development, allowing teams to deliver code changes more frequently and reliably. This chapter will cover the fundamental principles of configuring CI/CD pipelines specifically for Go applications, a language known for its simplicity, performance, and strong support for concurrent programming.

1. Understanding CI/CD ### 1.1 What is CI/CD?
CI is the practice of automatically testing and integrating code changes into a shared repository several times a day. It helps in detecting bugs early in the development cycle,

allowing teams to rectify issues before they escalate. CD builds on CI by automating the deployment of integrated changes to production environments. The primary objective is to create a seamless experience from code commit to deployment.

1.2 Benefits of CI/CD for Go Applications

Faster Feedback Loop: Developers receive immediate feedback on their code, allowing for quick iterations.
Higher Code Quality: Automated testing ensures that only well-tested code is deployed.
Consistency: Automated deployments reduce the risk of human errors and ensure consistent release processes.
Scalability: CI/CD practices can handle increasing amounts of traffic and user requests efficiently. ## 2. Setting Up Go Project Structure
Before diving into the configuration of CI/CD pipelines, it's important to establish a well-defined Go project structure. A typical Go application might look like this:

```
/my-go-appcmd
my-go-appmain.go
internal mypackage
handler.go handler_test.go
go.modgo.sum
```

In this structure:
`cmd` contains the application entry point.
`internal` contains the core application logic.
`go.mod` is the Go module file that specifies the

dependencies.## 3. Choosing a CI/CD Tool
There are several CI/CD tools available, tailored for Go projects. Some of the popular ones include:

GitHub Actions: A CI/CD service that integrates seamlessly within GitHub repositories.
GitLab CI: Built into GitLab, providing powerful pipelines and artifact management.
CircleCI: A cloud-based CI/CD tool that offers a highly configurable environment.
Travis CI: A popular hosted CI service that supports Go projects.

For this chapter, we'll demonstrate how to set up CI/CD pipelines using GitHub Actions, given its popularity and ease of use.

4. Configuring CI/CD Pipelines with GitHub Actions
4.1 Creating Your GitHub Actions Workflow
To get started with GitHub Actions:

Create a Workflow Directory: In your repository, create a directory named `.github/workflows`.

Set Up the CI Pipeline:

Create a YAML file (e.g., `ci.yaml`) inside the `.github/workflows` directory:

```yaml
name: Go CI

on:
  push:
```

```
branches: [ main ]pull_request:
branches: [ main ]

jobs:
build:
runs-on: ubuntu-lateststeps:
name: Checkout Code uses: actions/checkout@v2

name: Set Up Go
uses: actions/setup-go@v2with:
go-version: '1.19' # Specify your Go version

name: Install Dependenciesrun: go mod tidy

name: Run Testsrun: go test ./...
```

This configuration specifies that the CI pipeline will run on pushes and pull requests to the `main` branch. It checks out the code, sets up Go, installs dependencies, and executes tests.

4.2 Setting Up CD Deployment

Next, we'll set up continuous deployment to automatically deploy the application after successful tests. You could deploy to services like AWS, Google Cloud, or Heroku. Here's an example configuration for deploying a Go app to Heroku.

Add Heroku Authentication: You need to add your Heroku API key as a secret in the GitHub repository settings (Settings > Secrets > Actions).

Create a Deployment Step:

Update the `ci.yaml` file to include deployment steps:

```yaml
jobs:
build:
...

deploy:
runs-on: ubuntu-latest
needs: build # Ensures the build job completes successfully before deploying
steps:
- name: Checkout Code
  uses: actions/checkout@v2

  name: Set Up Go
  uses: actions/setup-go@v2
  with:
  go-version: '1.19'

  name: Deploy to Heroku
  env:
  HEROKU_API_KEY: ${{ secrets.HEROKU_API_KEY }}
  run: |
  git remote add heroku https://git.heroku.com/<your-heroku-app.git>
  git push heroku main
```

Replace `<your-heroku-app>` with your actual Heroku application name.

5. Testing the Pipeline

Now that you have your CI/CD pipeline set up, it's time to test it. Make a commit to the `main` branch, and observe GitHub Actions automatically running the defined workflows. If all tests pass, the application should be deployed seamlessly to Heroku.

6. Monitoring and Fault Tolerance

Though CI/CD pipelines automate much of the testing and deployment processes, monitoring and handling failures are equally critical. Use monitoring tools to track application performance and set up alerts for failures in your deployments. Additionally, consider implementing rollbacks in case of a failed deployment.

Configuring CI/CD pipelines is crucial for modern Go applications to ensure quality, speed, and efficiency in software delivery. By adopting CI/CD practices, teams can streamline their development processes and focus on what truly matters: building great software. As you embark on your CI/CD journey, remember to iterate on your pipeline configuration and adapt it based on your team's needs and feedback.

Conclusion

As we reach the end of our journey through "Web Applications with Go: Unlock the Power of Go for Real-World Web Server Development," it's essential to reflect on the knowledge and skills you've gained and to look forward to how you can apply them in your own projects.

Throughout this book, we've explored the fundamental aspects of web server development with Go, from understanding the language's core concepts and syntax to building robust, scalable web applications. The hands-on examples and practical tips provided throughout each chapter have been designed to equip you with the tools necessary to navigate the complexities of real-world projects confidently.

Go's simplicity, performance, and rich ecosystem make it an ideal choice for web development, whether you're creating small microservices or large-scale applications. You've learned how to leverage its powerful standard library, manage dependencies, handle routing, and implement middleware. Additionally, we discussed best practices for structuring your application, ensuring security, and optimizing performance, all of which are vital for building reliable and efficient web servers.

As you embark on your own web development projects, remember that the Go community is a wealth of resources and support. Engage with forums, contribute to open source, and continue learning from the extensive documentation available. The skills you've developed in this ebook are just the beginning—there is always more to discover and explore.

In closing, we hope this book has not only provided you with valuable insights and practical skills but also inspired you to dive deeper into the world of Go and web applications. Embrace the challenges ahead, continue to experiment, and never hesitate to push the boundaries of your knowledge. The power of Go is at your fingertips— unlock it, and build amazing web applications that can impact users and businesses alike.

Happy coding!

Biography

Tommy Clark is a passionate and dynamic author who combines a deep love for technology with an insatiable curiosity for innovation. As the mastermind behind the book *"Clark: A Journey Through Expertise and Innovation,"* Tommy brings years of hands-on experience in web development, web applications, and system administration to the forefront, offering readers a unique and insightful perspective.

With a strong background in Go programming and an ever-evolving fascination with crafting robust, efficient systems, Tommy excels at turning complex technical concepts into practical, actionable strategies. Whether building cutting-edge web solutions or diving into the intricate details of system optimization, Tommy's expertise is both broad and profound.

When not immersed in coding or writing, Tommy enjoys exploring the latest tech trends, tinkering with open-source projects, and mentoring aspiring developers. His enthusiasm for technology and dedication to empowering others shine through in everything he creates.

Join Tommy Clark on this exciting journey to unlock the full potential of technology—and get ready to be inspired, informed, and equipped to tackle your next big challenge!

Glossary: Web Applications with Go

A

API (Application Programming Interface): A set of rules and protocols that allows different software programs to communicate with each other. In web applications, APIs are often used to enable client-server interactions.

Authentication: The process of verifying the identity of a user or system. Common methods for authentication include username/password combinations, OAuth, and JWT (JSON Web Token).

B

Back-end: The server-side part of a web application that handles data storage, server logic, and communication with the database. In Go applications, the back-end typically consists of routes, database interactions, and business logic.

Bundler: A tool or library that helps manage dependencies in a Go project. It ensures that all necessary packages are included in the build process.

C

CRUD (Create, Read, Update, Delete): A set of four basic operations for managing data in applications. It represents the fundamental operations that can be performed on data in a database.

Context: A Go package that provides functionality for managing deadlines, cancellation signals, and request-scoped values. It is commonly used in web applications for handling requests and managing timeouts.

D

Database: A structured collection of data that can be easily accessed, managed, and updated. Common databases used with Go applications include PostgreSQL, MySQL, and MongoDB.

Dependency Injection: A design pattern used to promote loose coupling in your application, where an object or function receives its dependencies from an external source rather than creating them internally.

E

Embedded Filesystem: A method in Go for including files (like templates or static assets) within the compiled binary. This is useful for deploying self-contained applications without external file dependencies.

Environment Variable: A dynamic value that can affect the way running processes will behave on a computer. In web applications, environment variables are often used to store configuration settings such as database credentials and API keys.

F

Framework: A collection of libraries and tools that

provide a structure for building applications. Go has several frameworks for web development, including Gin, Echo, and Beego.

Frontend: The client-side part of a web application that users interact with directly. It includeseverything the user experiences in their browser, such as HTML, CSS, and JavaScript.

G

Goroutine: A lightweight thread managed by the Go runtime. Goroutines are used for concurrentprogramming and are ideal for handling multiple requests in a web application.

Middleware: A function that intercepts HTTP requests and responses to perform operations such as logging, authentication, and compression before passing control to the next handler.

H

HTTP (Hypertext Transfer Protocol): The foundation of data communication for the web. In Go, the `net/http` package is used to create web servers and handle HTTP requests.

Handler: A function in Go that processes HTTP requests and returns HTTP responses. Handlers are the core components of web applications.

J

JSON (JavaScript Object Notation): A lightweight data interchange format that is easy for humans to read and write. In web applications, JSON is commonly used for exchanging data between the server and the client.

JWT (JSON Web Token): A compact and self-contained means for securely transmitting information between parties as a JSON object. It is widely used for authentication and information exchange between the client and server.

L

Load Balancer: A system that distributes network or application traffic across multiple servers to ensure reliability and performance.

Logging: The practice of recording application events, errors, and other significant information to monitor performance, troubleshoot issues, and analyze usage patterns.

M

MVC (Model-View-Controller): A software design pattern used for developing user interfaces by dividing an application into three interconnected components. It separates the internal representations of information from the ways that information is presented and accepted by the user.

Microservices: An architectural style that structures

an application as a collection of loosely coupled services, which communicate over APIs. Go is often used for building microservices due to its simplicity and performance.

R

Routing: The process of mapping HTTP requests to specific handler functions based on the request URL and method. In Go, routing is typically handled using a router or framework.

S

Static Files: Files that are served to the client without any modification, such as CSS, JavaScript, images, and fonts. In Go, static files can be served using the `http.FileServer` function.

Struct: A composite data type in Go that groups together variables (fields) under a single name. Structs are commonly used to model complex data structures, such as user profiles and database records.

T

Template: A file that defines a layout with placeholders for data. Go's `html/template` package allows developers to generate dynamic HTML content based on templates.

Testing: The process of evaluating a program by running it under specified conditions to verify that it behaves as expected. Go provides built-in support for writing and running tests.

U

URL (Uniform Resource Locator): The address used to access resources on the Internet. In web applications, URLs are often constructed to define routes and parameters.

V

Version Control: A system that records changes to files or sets of files over time so that you can recall specific versions later. Git is the most popular version control system used in Go development.